© 2010 by Design Media Publishing Limited
This edition published in May 2011

Design Media Publishing Limited
20/F Manulife Tower
169 Electric Rd, North Point
Hong Kong
Tel: 00852-28672587
Fax: 00852-25050411
E-mail: Kevinchoy@designmediahk.com
www.designmediahk.com

Editing: Yeal Xie
Proofreading: Maggie Wang, Katy Lee
Design/Layout: Hai CHI

ISBN 978-988-19738-3-2

Printed in China

Spas
Holiday Resorts

Edited by Yeal Xie

DESIGN MEDIA PUBLISHING LIMITED

Contents

SPA

Tamina Thermal Baths

Location:
Zürich, Switzerland

Designer:
Joseph Smolenicky

Photographer:
Walter Mair

Completion date:
2009

The Tamina Thermal Baths is explicitly conceived as a part of the grand-hotel culture. The cultural and aesthetic identity of the project seeks an affinity to both Swiss tradition and the grand hotels of the Baltic coast. For this reason the building volume has a monumental character, in order to stand out as an institution equal to the other buildings in the resort. Simultaneously the thermal baths are intended to relativise the almost "urban" stonework character of the spa spring hall.

This strategy of using an explicit resort architecture is underscored in the building's formally fanciful oval windows. Seen from the inside, the windows have the effect of over-dimensional picture frames. Oval picture frames were widespread in the Victorian era for landscape scenes, whereby the intention in the current project is to give specific expression to the view over the relatively neutral landscape by means of the gesture of the frame.

Metaphorically the creation of the interior spaces of the project has an analogy in cutting clearings in the pattern of a forest by felling individual trees. This is the reverse of the common design process. The exterior spaces are similarly created by "felling" supports on the periphery of the building volume. Structurally the building can be more or less seen as a forest, created out of columns instead of trees – a total of 115 supports using the timber of 2,200 fir-trees.

1.The magnificent building
2.The building and the landscape fuse together, showing a vacation atmosphere
3.The white columns look like trees in a forest
4.The landscape is as beautiful as a painting
5.The interior decoration with white as the main palette is elegant and pure
6.One can enjoy full relaxation in the bath pool
7.The oval windows look like picture frames

Materially the project possesses the same appearance internally and externally. The snow-white timber battens are carried over internally as wall surfacing. In this sense there is no actual interior architecture to the building, but instead only a whole architecture of the building.

The timber structure of the building is not merely determined by the criteria of the span of the supports. Instead of a focus on the engineering of the function of the supports and the reinforcement of a construction, the structure concentrates far more on spatial phenomena, creating a beauty and a ceremonial atmosphere. Bathing is celebrated as a cultivated activity.

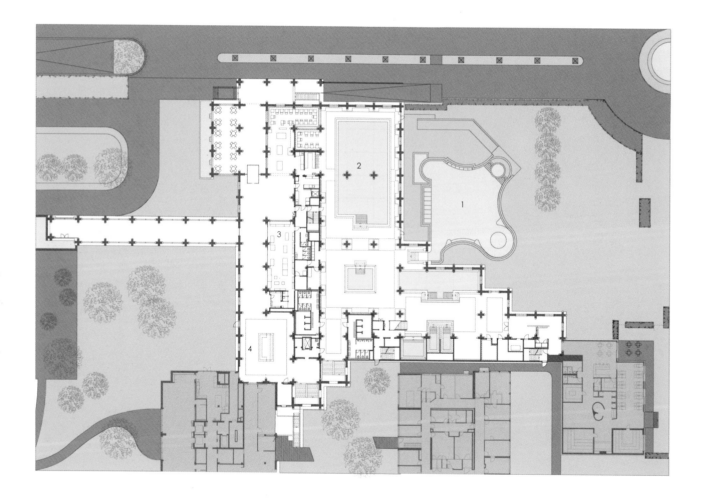

1. Outdoor bath pool
2. Indoor bath pool
3. Treatment room
4. Lounge

3

Merano Thermal Baths

Location:
South Tyrol, Italy

Designer:
Matteo Thun & Partners

Completion date:
2007

Recreation, harmony and relaxation are among the main aims in the Merano Thermal Baths, featuring a total of 25 pools and a refined sauna area. Here the bather will find all he can wish for, from a refreshing cold plunge pool and hot whirlpools to relaxing brine pools. A special inside-outside feeling is provided in the big pool, where the bather can start indoors and simply swim out to a fascinating mountain scenery!

Cosy warmth and a unique flair are provided by a first-class sauna area. Here guests may relax, unwind and sweat while contemporaneously boosting their immune system. Among the state-of-the-art facilities are a Finnish sauna, two steam baths, a sanarium, hay bath, caldarium and an outdoor log cabin sauna. After taking the sauna, the guests can look forward to several cold dips and a very special way of cooling off – in the snow room, where it snows from the ceiling and they will feel like being in the midst of South Tyrol's eternal glaciers.

In 26 treatment rooms people can indulge in the most different kinds of baths, from milk and honey baths to vinotherapy baths for two and the relaxing mountain pine baths. This is the place to relax, and this is the place to unwind.

The green heart of the Merano Thermal Baths is a stunning park, covering an area of more than 50,000 square metres. 478 different kinds of roses, 900 water lilies and historic old trees render the park a wonderful spot and the ideal place to relax.

1.Merano Thermal Baths at night
2.The large bath pool connects the
interior and exterior spaces
3.The exterior part of the pool
4.The outdoor bath pool is divided by
black paths
5.The plant decoration in the indoor
bath pool creates a natural environment
6.The bathtub
7.The glass screen makes the whole
spa natural and transparent

3

Shangri-La's Rasa Sayang Resort and Spa, Penang

Location:
Penang, Malaysia

Designer:
One Plus Partnership Limited

Photographer:
One Plus Partnership Limited

Completion date:
2008

The Spa at Shangri-La's Rasa Sayang Resort and Spa, Penang has won the "Best Spa Design" and "Best Spa Therapist" at the highly regarded Malaysia Spa and Wellness Awards 2008.

Set amid 30 acres of lush tropical greenery with the comfort of year-round sun, sand and ocean breezes, Shangri-La's Rasa Sayang Resort and Spa offers 304 luxurious guestrooms and suites in its Rasa Wing and Garden Wing. Each of the rooms, and the resort's signature roof in particular, incorporate aesthetic influences of the Minangkabau, an indigenous tribe that originates from West Sumatra in Indonesia, through an extensive use of carved wood, traditional textures and colourful fabrics.

Rasa Premier Rooms provide spatial elegance and custom-crafted furnishing that creates an exotic yet familiar living environment, coupled with oversized, deep-soak balcony bathtubs that provide an extra touch of relaxation. Rasa Deluxe Rooms feature private verandas with private garden space and are ideal for an exotic retreat.

Art and artefacts crafted by local and regional artisans are displayed prominently around the resort, including in its food and beverage outlets such as Spice Market Café. However, the art and artefacts are more than just decoration; they are narratives of a time when culture, art and tradition were an integral part

1.The resort has beautiful natural environment
2.Nature is blended into every corner of the resort
3.The outdoor bath pool is surrounded by trees
4.The simple and generous lobby
5.The interior bath pool in the sunlight
6.The interior decoration combines Malaysian culture
7.The comfortable guestroom design
8.The guestroom has complete functions

of the old way of life in the tribal and local Malay communities.

In essence, the decorative aspects of Shangri-La's Rasa Sayang Resort and Spa celebrate the rich diversity of Malaysian art, culture, tradition and heritage, which are complemented by the warmth of the resort's service team, renowned for its Malaysian hospitality.

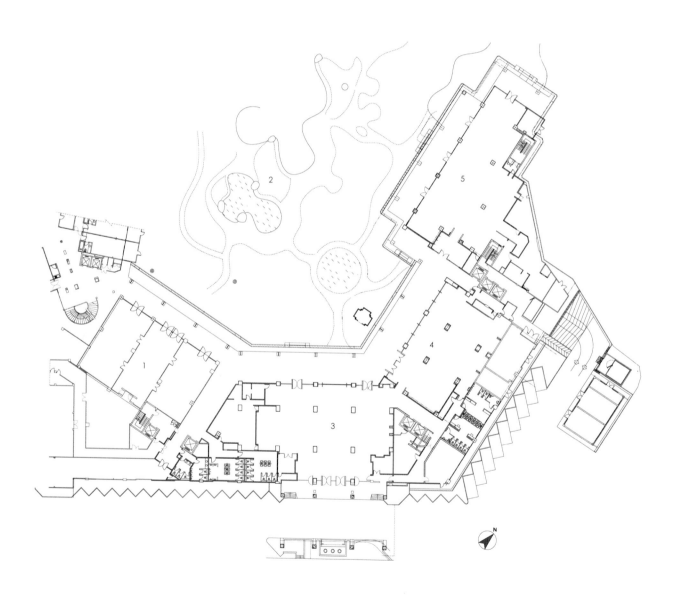

1. Treatment room
2. Swimming pool
3. Waiting area
4. Lounge
5. Café

3

4

Aramsa Spa

Location:
Singapore

Designer:
Formwerkz

Photographer:
Formwerkz

Completion date:
2007

The site sits on approximately 6,000 square metres of park land in Bishan, surrounded by densely populated housing estates. The existing cluster of seven single-storey retail buildings scattered around the site are converted to accommodate an integrated day spa facility. Despite the exclusivity of the spa furctions, the spa complex is to engage the public and park users in its activities wherever possible. This creates a dichotomy between the public and private realms, as the insertion of an integrated spa facility in a public park is by itself a privatisation of public space. However, the project attempts to publicise its private realms to a large extent without giving up on privacy and exclusivity totally. This is achieved by creating visual links into the inner sanctions of the spa through transparent intermediate spaces and layers of lush gardens that sandwich the various pockets of spa components. The sensitive selection of plant palette helps to give the much preferred privacy where needed most.

Diagrammatically, a network of curves is superimposed over the grid of the existing structures, slicing the compound into distinct zones, as a programmatic and circulation parti. The curves form stratums of spaces, with the zones filtering through the curved layers with increasing levels of privacy. At the main entrance, a sweeping curve dressed in a façade of creepers, seems to have emerged

1. The spa is surrounded by dense greenery
2. The plants divide the space for privacy
3. Is it a spa in plants or a spa with plants?
4. The detail design of interior decoration is also close to nature
5. In the sun, guests can have a rest surrounded by plants

from the ground. This grand and yet sensitive gesture for the most public part of the spa addresses its relationship to the domain of the public park.

The different stratums of spaces are interspersed with distinctive gardens also defined by the curves. The spaces are all extroverted with views out to the interspersed gardens, "extending" the landscape into the interiors. Within some interiors, trees and plants literally emerged into spaces. As one circulates through the spaces, one is constantly viewing gardens in the foreground while silvers of openings and lattices in the curved walls suggest other interspersed gardens in the background and the private stratums beyond.

The extension of nature is not just restricted to narratives but also extended into appendages: standing lamps are shaped like potted plants, giant bulb-shaped chandeliers covered in green, larger-than-life garden-lights shaped like luminous pebbles that glow in the evenings.

1. Gym
2. Reception
3. Spa retail
4. Lounge
5. Staff office
6. Treatment room

Thermal Bath, Therapy and Hotel, Bad Gleichenberg

Location:
Bad Gleichenberg, Austria

Designer:
Jensen & Skodvin Arkitektkontor AS

Photographer:
Jensen & Skodvin Arkitektkontor AS

Completion date:
2008

The project is situated in a protected park and consists of a treatment area with about 50 different rooms for medical treatments, a four-star hotel with several different restaurants and cafés, and a public thermal bath for the patients and other guests.

The waiting areas in the middle of the treatment rooms for the patients are shaped around courtyards allowing sun and views to the trees, as to give the patients the impression of waiting in the park itself. A full treatment might last for several days and can consist of a number of different treatments, like different types of massages and baths in smaller private treatment rooms, a visit to a cold room with minus 110 degrees Celsius, etc. Between these treatments the patients wait in the open and transparent waiting areas where the park is always close.

The designers wanted to create a low building with a series of gardens, giving light and creating a sense of privacy and exclusion, while at the same time opening up for some of the spectacular views. The wind bracing was exercised using a very simple rule. Where the engineer wanted bracing, the designers always made a connection from one node on the floor level, to the next node on the roof level. Because of all the different dimensions in the plan this creates correspondingly different angles for the bracing, which, because it has the same size as the pillar, is always visible.

1.The "sky garden" on the first floor
2.The swimming pool on the ground floor can be seen from the first-floor terrace
3.The flowers are in full bloom
4.The exterior swimming pool under the trees
5.People can enjoy the fresh air even in the interior
6.The night view
7.The natural environment makes people peaceful

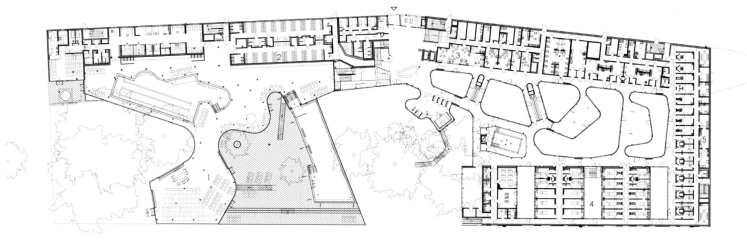

1. Platform
2. Dressing room
3. Relaxation room
4. Treatment room
5. Office

3

4

5

Spa and Wellness Facilities at Elounda

Location:
Elounda, Greece

Designer:
Davide Macullo

Completion date:
2007

The refurbishment of the penthouse for a new spa in Elounda Beach Resort gives the opportunity to treat the indoor and outdoor spaces as a whole, thus increasing the perception of the space and the feeling of "floating" over the amazing landscape. The "white boxes", that host the different functions, give the whole an harmonious structure increasing the visual continuity between internal and external spaces that go beyond the physical boundaries to extend towards the sea and the hills of Creta; nature seems to enter the spa and draws a new artificial scenery. The project aims at granting a sense of lightness and freshness to meet the prerogatives of a place in which soul and body are treated. The interior spaces, characterised by the use of "light" materials such as glass and translucent panels for walls and ceilings, create a visual neutral continuity and effects of reflections, while the surrounding landscape dominates the space and sheds its colours. The essentiality of the materials and the graphic sign of the "leaves" pattern contribute to stretch the perspective throughout an atmosphere of pastel colours and lightness, emphasised by the use of indirect artificial lighting at night.

1.The spa is surrounded by landscapes
2.The bath pool is decorated with
leaf-shaped pattern
3.The screen with leaf-shaped pattern
4.The clean and open lobby
5.The products area
6.The outdoor swimming pool
7.The leaf-shaped pattern can be
seen everywhere

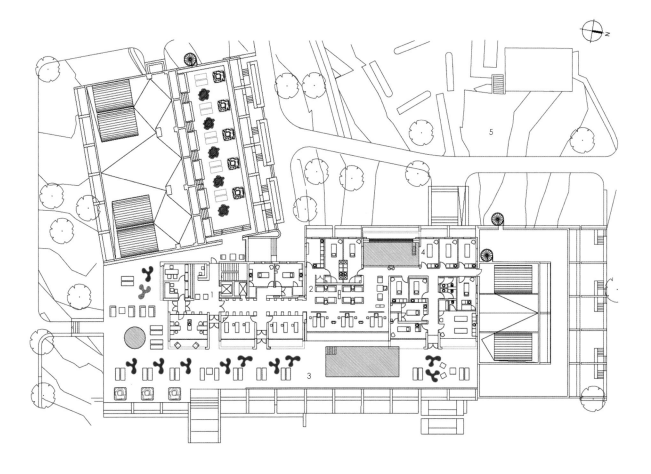

1. Treatment area
2. Beauty salon
3. Outdoor bath pool
4. Indoor bath pool
5. Swimming pool

3

4

5

Spa Furama

Location:
Singapore

Designer:
Formwerkz

Photographer:
Jeremy San

Completion date:
2008

To create a design that transcends boundaries – that was the brief given by the client Furama International, in line with their plan to grow the new spa and hotel chain worldwide. The spa is envisioned to be a seamless experience, a space without straight, dingy corridors leading to the individual rooms and rooms without corners. The circle is the first, the simplest and the most perfect form. The circle became the chosen form to create a strong and fluid space. It was a site response to the huge columns and service ducts that marked the inner component of the spa located on the 5th storey pool deck level of Furama Riverfront. To heighten the experience of the circular forms and the residual spaces outside the circles, the predominant colour palette was kept to the purest of shades – white. White, when rendered with materials of different transparency, becomes the most intriguing backdrops for play of coloured lights and silhouettes.

Due to the limited floor area, the single rooms are conceived as cocoons that can be easily reconfigured to combine into double rooms whenever the need arises. The level of privacy can also be adjusted by the different layering of curvilinear skins. Even the outdoor cabanas, which offer a more tropical environment for spa treatments, are enclosed with rotating envelopes and circular folding screens which become lit lanterns amidst the landscape

1.The entrance
2.Circular pattern is repeatedly used in the design
3.The bath pool is also dotted with plants
4.The circular private room
5.The separated circular semi-private room
6.The treatment room

of the pool deck at night. Interesting interior details include the subtle incorporation of bath elements like shower hose and water pipes of various diameters throughout the spa.

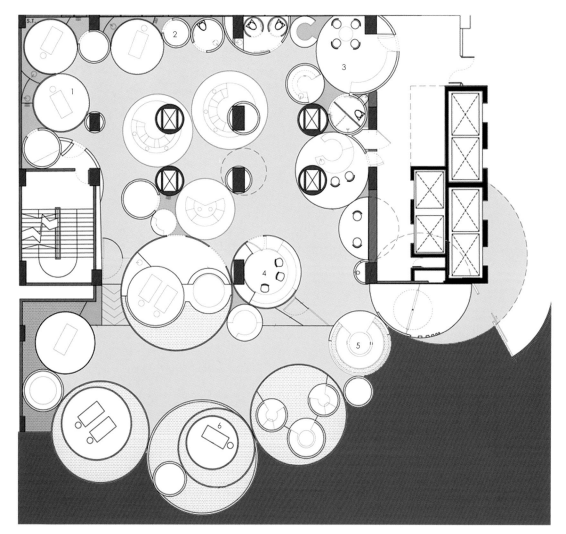

1. Massage room
2. Steam bath
3. Staff room
4. Reception
5. Lounge
6. Outdoor bath pool

Banyan Tree Spa Sanya

Location:
Sanya, China

Designer:
Banyan Tree Group
Architrave Design & Planning

Completion date:
2008

The Spa extends a luxurious welcome to visitors, presenting the epitome of a romantic getaway by the pristine fine beaches of Hainan Island. Home to eight lavish treatment pavilions, it offers an oasis of peace and tranquility where guests may indulge in a series of award-winning signature treatments while taking in the breathtaking views of lush hills and beaches.

True to form, the spa is a visual study in understated tropical cool. It's a resort focal point and dispenses quality treatments and spa packages. Black slate backdrops public areas along with a mix of natural fabrics and wood. A brief foot ritual is a prelude to most treatments as well as the usual popular menu items. Sanya also offers two-hour-plus packages and boasts a state-of-the-art hydrotherapy area. Under the guidance of staff, those who want to get wet are steered through a sequence of hot and cold-water experiences: Rain Shower Corridors, Steam Rooms, Ice Fountains and Jet Pools, a process that is said to benefit blood circulation by expanding and contracting capillaries alternately.

Banyan Tree Sanya is China's first all-pool villa resort and sets accommodation around a narrow lagoon in its own privately accessed

2

3

1.The spa is close to nature
2.The waterscape in the lobby
3.The peaceful environment for a vacation
4.Each detail design has different flavours
5.The outdoor treatment area

bay. All pool gardens are well designed for seclusion and a large alfresco bathtub is set in a small lily pond off the villa bathroom. Food from its Thai, international and Chinese kitchen can be enjoyed from the comfort of the villa and downtown Sanya is a mere 15-minute cab-ride.

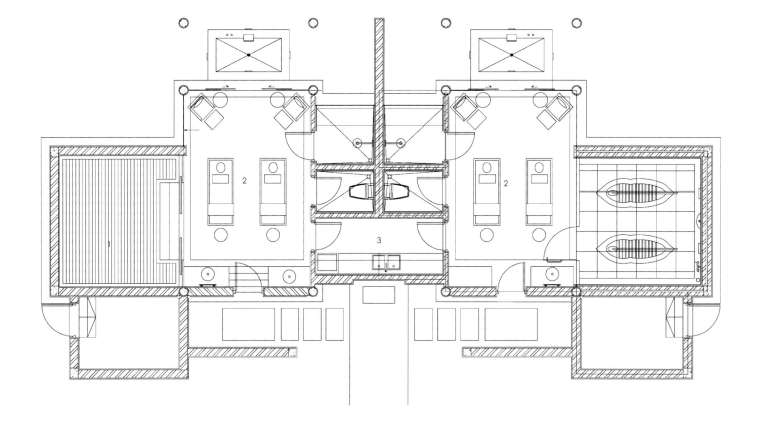

1. Platform
2. Treatment room
3. Steam room

4

5

Baths at Panticosa

Location:
Huesca, Spain

Designer:
Moneo Brock Studio SL

Photographer:
Jeff Brock, Luis Asin

Completion date:
2008

The older development of the spa seemed to deny the real situation of the springs, thus the designers sought from the very beginning to reaffirm the wilderness of the place in the architecture; they wished to give the mountain back its voice. More than just acknowledging the natural landscape that surrounds the building, they wanted to make it a player in the architecture.

In the interior design they were looking for an effect of light, views, and a fluid internal relationship of spaces that would draw visitors through the installations, encouraging a sense of discovery rather than that of a programmed itinerary, encouraging a meandering kind of experience where the nature of one's "ailment" and its "treatment" may be one's own to discover.

The municipal zoning limits require that much of the floor area be located underground, making the provision of natural light and views of the natural surroundings to the maximum area of the plan a design priority. Glass blocks were employed to bring light to the building interiors, which faced the mountain on all sides, and to express luminosity to the exterior at the same time. By using different combinations of translucent wall, vision glass, and screen walls made of columns of glass blocks, views of the surrounding landscape were modulated to provide just the right amount of light and orienting cues for the visitors inside.

1. The spa is surrounded by mountains
2. White is the main theme of the interior design
3. The use of glass and screen makes the interior lighting comfortable and natural
4. The snow mountains can be seen from the interior
5. Sunlight comes into the spacious lobby
6. The treatment room
7. The interior design makes guests feel as if they were in a natural space

Fountains and reflecting pools were designed around the south and west sides of the building to amplify the daylight shining on and into the building. To bring daylight and mountain views into the centre of the plan and down to the lower levels, the building mass was made to embrace the mountain, and the façade sections between terraces were crenellated.

Within the building, spatial arrangements are very complex, and the partitioning of the plans somewhat labyrinthine, with repetitive and circular patterns of circulation, twists and turns of walls and a multiplicity of interconnected levels. However, the consistency of the design language, and the possibility of making repeated reference to the different mountain peaks give visitors a sense of where they are in the building at all times, and a sense of its organisation.

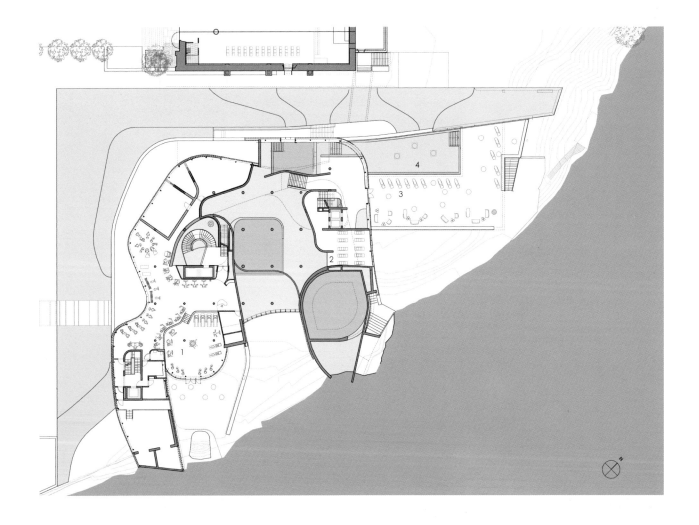

1. Gym
2. Lounge hydrotherapy
3. Relaxation lounge
4. Outdoor pool

Exedra Nice Hotel Wellness Centre

Location:
Nice, France

Designer:
Simone Micheli

Photographer:
Jürgen Eheim

Completion date:
2008

Inside the famous Hotel Exedra Nice in Nice, property of Boscolo Hotels, in the basement ground rises the amazing wellness centre, signed by the architect Simone Micheli. "Planning a space designed for the psycho-physical regeneration and recreational relax, in the beautiful Costa Azzurra, means to converse with the existing historical background through the creation of emotional and anti-mimetic places connected to our contemporaneity, seduced by the will to exalt the senses of the guests through a project with strong and exciting features that develop into sinestesya. A new step towards the future according to my architectural belief and my content and formal benchmarks, for excellent dreams and realisations" (Simone Micheli).

Everything is designed to include and cherish the guest in this dream: a new wellness centre able to live even independently from the hotel. We cross the spaces walking on a rough flooring in natural Prun stone, and set against the plasticity of everything that's around us; we can find the clean and essential furnishings and the ceiling coloured by the hole in the ceiling. Fluid shop-windows for cosmetics, internally painted blue, emerge quite naturally from the shaped walls and from the ground, lighted with white 1W-led spotlights like a mighty white tree/sculpture erects almost casually into the defined spaces. Going on in this sensorial path, curvy and harmonic shapes transpose

1.The reception
2.The curve design in the front makes the space soft and beautiful
3.Curtains are used as partitions
4.The bathing pool looks like a fairyland
5.The gym
6.The clean interior environment
7.The tap resembles a tree

themselves in a fluid covering "curtain effect", realised in expanded polyurethane and finished with plaster and shiny white resin, that characterises the corridors and all the wellness area. This space is completed by a wide double cabin for couple treatments with a long bathtub in white solid surface.

Going on, we can find the wet zone of the centre: steam bath, aromatic showers, vichy showers, ice maker, cold and hot waters, that offer the customer a deep dive in a dimension that allows to relax in a dreaming and unreal atmosphere. In the end emerges the extraordinary space of the pool-whirpool bath with its covering in glassed mosaic tiles that wraps the wall covering, generating a fluid fragment of sky, thanks to the thin and punctual blue luminescence of the built-in LEDs and to the continuous reflections of the water on the move. The pool, dominated by the big

idealised tree, from which the branch comes out a strong massaging throw of water, presents a long lateral seat with whirlpool bath, covered with a silver glassed mosaic, and inside rise several effects and water plays. Scenographic waterfalls come down from a huge intense blue metallic portal, that marks the main entrance to the pool, from a wide disc in shiny stainless steel put on the ceiling and from the big wall showers backlit with blue light, making unique and exclusive this spectacular wellness path into the water.

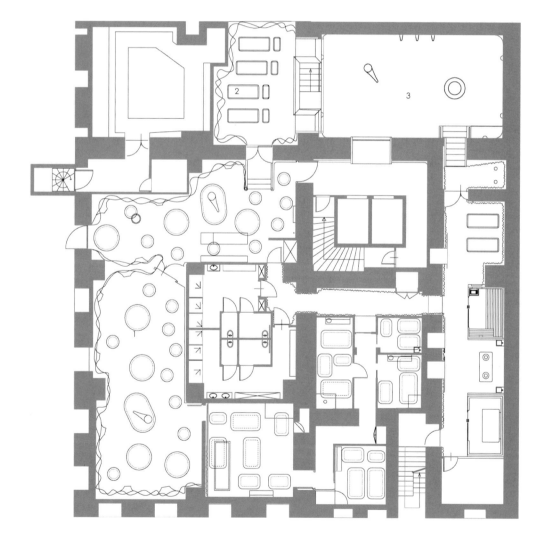

1. Bath area
2. Treatment room
3. Bath pool

4

5

Oulton Hall Hotel Spa

Location:
Leeds, England

Designer:
Greyline Design

Consultant Architect:
3DReid

Photographer:
Cloud 9

Completion date:
2008

Oulton Hall Hotel in Leeds is part of the De Vere Collection and is the only five star hotel and spa facility in Yorkshire, England. The project has included the extensive refurbishment of the main reception, bar and restaurant area, to provide high-quality dining and leisure facilities. The refurbishment of the spa, meanwhile, provides state-of-the-art facilities including a gym, fitness studio, a 15-metre-long heated swimming pool, a Jacuzzi and treatment room facilities. Within all of the refurbished areas, the attention to detail is superb with finishing touches that enhance the product and offer guests a feeling of luxury throughout.

One of the greatest challenges was improving the flow of the public spaces which was somewhat disjointed. This involved relocating the bar and creating a new Champagne bar offering. The hotel now has far greater flexibility from these rooms, and leisure guests and business guests can be kept apart more easily. All of the furnishings are bespoke, unique to Oulton Hall. The lines are very elegant while the fabrics are sumptuous silks and velvets, and much lighter than one would normally expect. Colour-wise, rich tones of gold and taupe predominate in the main public areas; the bar is accented in varying shades of blue while the restaurant is a dramatic Chinese red with black-lacquered detailing.

1.The central bath pool
2.The chairs along the staircase
3.The interior design is classic and elegant
4.The fabrics of silks and velvets are comfortable and luxurious
5.The central bath pool has a view of the surrounding rooms
6.The washstand in the treatment room
7.The treatment room provides complete facilities and good services
8.A corner of the treatment room

It was key for the designers to take the style they had developed in the public rooms through into the spa area, though they made it slightly moodier, with punches of dark copper colour for drama. They retained only the pool hall, which is simplified and screened off with an elegant dark wood and glass screen, and most other areas had to be completely re-planned to make the spa flow well.

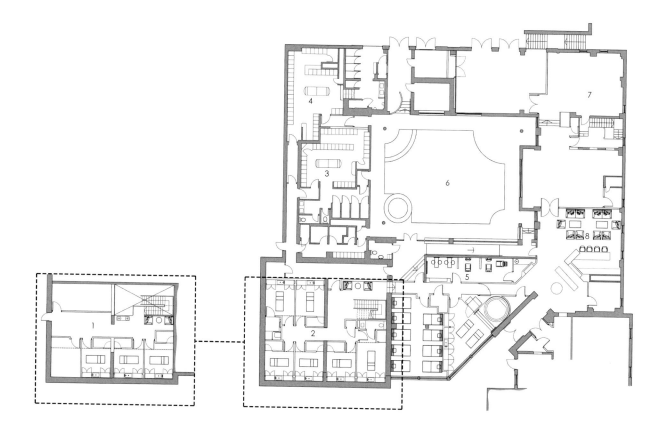

1. The treatment area on the first floor
2. The treatment area on the ground floor
3. Female dressing room
4. Male dressing room
5. Beauty salon
6. Swimming pool
7. Gym
8. Juice bar

3

4

5

6

7

8

Hyatt Key West Resort & Spa

Location:
Key West, USA

Designer:
morrisonseifertmurphy

Photographer:
morrisonseifertmurphy

Completion date:
2008

This newly renovated Key West resort is taking the Key West experience to a new level. The renovation has transformed the property into a truly "tropical modern" experience, a unique environment like no other in Key West. The hotel has been transformed into an intimate spa-like facility with the use of light colours along with crisp detailing. A clean soothing material palette greets you in the renovated lobby and also connects to the pool lounge/deck area and the new spa treatment rooms. The 118 rooms have been updated to have a clean, fresh and timeless appearance and are unexpected surprise with a tropical modern quality.

As the guests walk into the guestrooms, they immediately sense the cooling effect of the white tile floors. The use of the light-coloured bamboo along with other natural finishes provides the backdrop for the colourful accent fabrics and artwork found in the rooms. The bathrooms have a spa-like quality with light finishes and unique plumbing fittings. Since the baths open directly to the rooms, they act as an extension of the room with their aqua glass mosaic accent wall and open layout. During the day natural light fills the bath and at night the accent lighted glass mosaic wall adds a dramatic feature to the room.

1.In the spa, guests will feel at home
2.One can have a rest in the outdoor
natural environment
3.The professional spa facilities
4.The interior and exterior spaces are
connected
5.The guestroom and the bathroom
are connected
6.A complete set of bath facilities

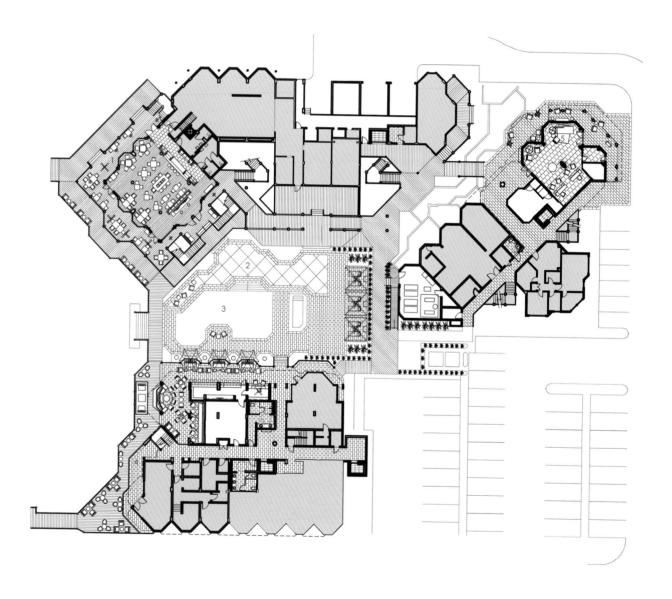

1. Restaurant
2. Treatment area
3. Bath pool
4. Relaxation area
5. Lobby

4

5

Carbon Hotel Spa

Location:
Genk, Belgium

Designer:
Peter Cornoedus

Photographer:
Peter Cornoedus

Completion date:
2008

Carbon Hotel Spa offers a health club, sauna, hammam, chromotherapy, relaxation treatments, massage, cocoon corners, herbal baths, Tai Chi and Chakra and a large south-facing terrace. The first-floor terrace garden of the hotel is a calm sanctuary in the middle of bustling Genk. In a dark and sober shades ranging from grey to black slate, parts of the hotel recall us of the shades of coal. The 60 rooms are spacious and equipped with all the latest hi-tech and in their bathrooms with extra large showers and huge tubs. Simple lines and materials chosen emphasise the natural beauty: the natural beauty of the planet and also yours. The hotel spa will provide you with care in this spirit. The scrubs, massages and Tai Chi and Chakra classes are proposed to allow people to be in harmony with the body, gently soothe themselves and find the true nature.

The wellness experience is part of the vibrant rejuvenation of the commercial centre of Genk, the heart of the 19th-century Limburg coal-mining industry. The Carbon dedicates itself to life's vital element in both name and design.

1.The first-floor terrace uses mirrors as decoration
2.The first-floor terrace is a calm sanctuary in the bustling city
3.The terrace leading to the first floor
4.The grey and black colours make people sober and calm
5.The design is open and simple
6.One can rest or meditate in the corner
7.The fresh storage room

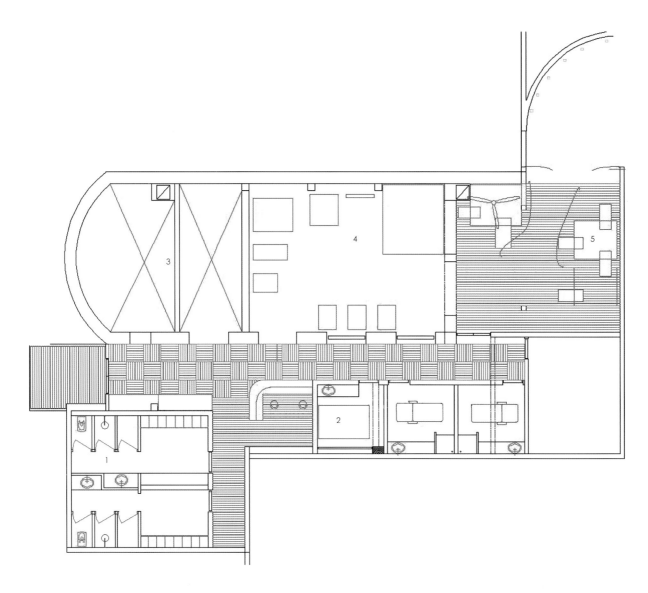

1. Dressing room
2. Massage bed
3. Beauty salon
4. Treatment room
5. Lounge

Hotel Europe Spa

Location:
Killarney, Ireland

Designer:
Hirsch Bedner Associates

London Director:
Inge Moore

Photographer:
Hirsch Bedner Associates

Completion date:
2008

The Gallery, Hirsch Bedner Associates' London-based studio, has added another feather to its cap with the striking redesign of Hotel Europe.

Hotel Europe has one of Ireland's most comprehensive spa facilities, managed by world-class operator ESPA. In creating the spa, guests are greeted in the spa lobby by an impressive art installation of carved monolithic timber blocks spread along the floor, echoing design features from the hotel lobby. During the day, an 11-metre-tall glass-enclosed atrium staircase floods the entry area with warm daylight. The wall flanking the staircase is composed of dark water, and in the grey afternoon hours, a central glass chandelier casts warm spirals of light from above the stair. Upon arrival to the spa, guests are visually engaged with a century-old Irish pattern, cut out from paper-thin bronze sheets suspended from the ceiling. Spa amenities are comprised on two separate levels. The first, or active level contains a state-of-the-art fitness, kinesis and Tai Chi studio, along with female and male changing rooms.

This active level has opalescent silk wall coverings and jewel-like creamish grey accents that contrast with the dark and opulent relaxation areas. Here, the hardness of the black stonewall, dappled with niches for candlelight, is complemented and softened by velvet throws and soft pillows, while custom-

1.The custom-made rest bed
2.The velvet fabrics, the printing wallpaper and the grey and white tone all bring a taste of nobility
3.Guests can enjoy full relaxation in the world of water
4.The semi-transparent soft screen

designed bespoke relaxation beds surrounded by slat sail-like screens offer the ultimate privacy and comfort. Also on this level is a plunge pool adjacent to the indoor/outdoor vitality pool, plus a brasserie and "heat experience" areas consisting of a salt-water vitality pool, steam room, sauna and large activity showers in dark, dramatic tones.

The second floor is more of a sanctuary, offering treatment rooms arranged around a peaceful internal courtyard that is designed as a contemporary topiary garden. The tone here is sleek and sophisticated, with silver ash timber flooring, warm greys and lacquered surfaces. Bespoke-patterned metal panels, original B&B Italia armchairs upholstered in soft, opulent charcoal grey velvet and Mercury silver art give guests the ultimate setting for decadent pampering and treatments. This level also features a private terraced suite, complete with a Wenge-wood sauna overlooking the lake, sizable rain showers, and a stone-clad tub with water jets for two.

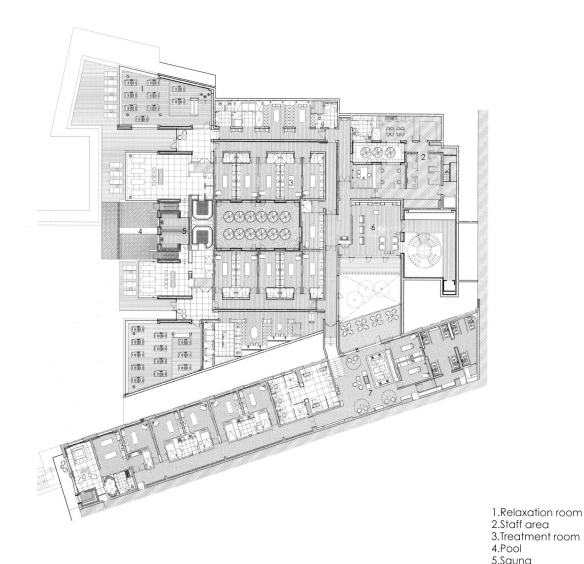

1.Relaxation room
2.Staff area
3.Treatment room
4.Pool
5.Sauna
6.Reception
7.Lounge

3

4

Wald & Schlosshotel Friedrichsruhe Spa

Location:
Friedrichsruhe, Germany

Designer:
niki szilagyi interior architecture

Completion date:
2008

After crossing the large lobby, a perfect place for exhibitions or events, the entrance to the spa next to the reception is kept narrow to surprise the guest with a gorgeous view of the spacious pool area. The swimming hall with gallery extends to the first floor and is flooded with daylight – due to the roof light.

Different themes are shown in the saunas and steam baths. An imposing feature serves on the one hand as a towel shelf – on the other hand as an illuminated partition. Adjacent to it you will find a water bar with silver quartzite flagstones. A booth consisting of a steam bath, sauna, showers and space for relaxation is located at the back of this area. It can be used exclusively for a group of women, for example. Directly from the sauna area, the outdoor facilities with the kelo sauna, a kneipp-pond and a jacuzzi can be reached. Inside you can lounge on comfortable furniture, whereas outside you can relax on a wooden bench under a huge bonsai.

In Sauna area, the silver quartzite continues down the generous stairs with illuminated steps and into the gallery, where the relaxation rooms with different design themes are located. In the room of total relaxation you sink in a crème-coloured world of cushions. The library with its open fire is designed with warm colours and has specially-made divan beds with reading lamps. This room is the perfect place to read at leisure. The third relaxation room is very light thanks to its fanlight.

1. The bathtub and sofa
2. The exquisitely designed foot spa facility
3. The treatment room
4. The circulation space is used for storage too

A large part of the treatment area is also floored with lime stone. In the treatment rooms precious walnut parquet is used to transmit a feeling of warmth. The furniture is also made of walnut to reduce the amount of different materials to create a room of silence and relaxation. An impressive light field was designed together with Johannes Klinger. A poetic shadow play is created with silver wine leaves bedded in acryl. Designed in a more masculine way, the men's suites have a wengè-accent.

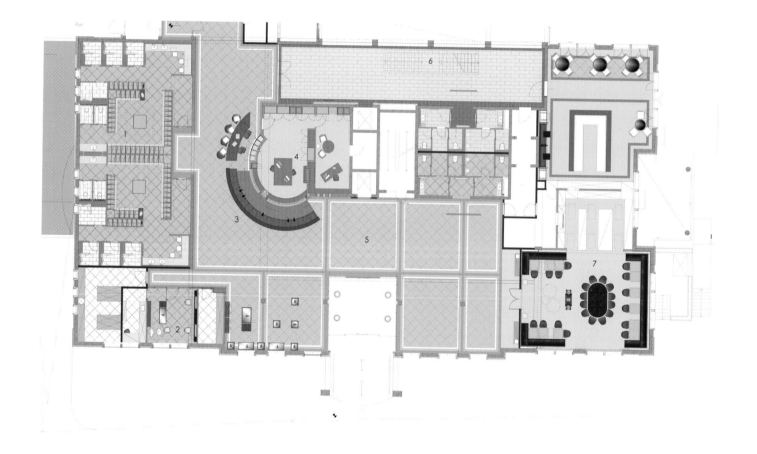

1. Dressing room
2. Treatment room
3. Reception
4. Office
5. Lounge
6. Bath pool
7. Foot spa

3

4

Roomers Hotel Spa

Location:
Frankfurt, Germany

Designer:
3deluxe-biorhythm and Grübel

Photographer:
Ernst Stratmann

Completion date:
2009

From the outside of the building you can see the classic architectural lines that burrow a highlight: the innovative glass roof of the spectacular Conference & Spa facilities.

The concept is formed out of the 3C, contemplative work and listening in the conference area, communication and celebrations in the sky lounge and then the conclusion and confident, sexy perception in the relaxed and inspirational atmosphere of the spa.

A roundly shaped sauna is surrounded with floating and interchanging lights. A steam bath with sensual lighting and a glass crystal beach with lighting objects, which resemble mysterious jelly fish. The relaxing water jet beds facing at the nylon ceiling are another highlight. This all is completed by the massage pool with changing lights and a transparent foliation at the veneer. The gym with its smart reflection on all sides and the dynamic lights create a positive atmosphere of movement. The outside terrace is like the whole spa project, elegant, laminated and soundproof. The spa area is open to all hotel guests.

1.The bar with mirror decoration
2.One can enjoy full relaxation in the spa
3.The light fixture above the bathtub
has a fantastic effect
4.The steam room

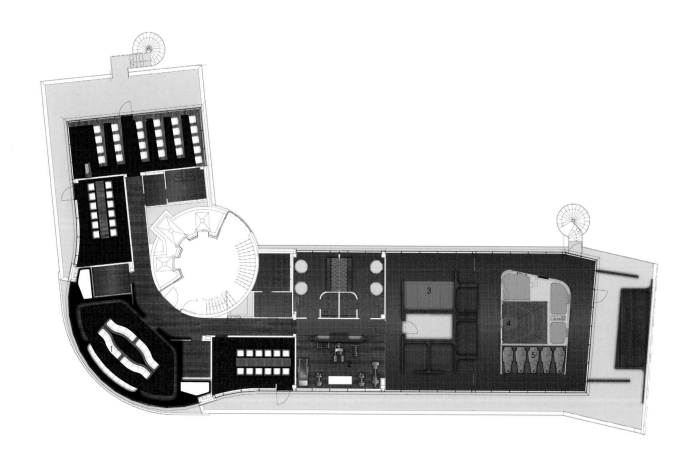

1. Lounge
2. Beauty salon
3. Bath pool
4. Steam room
5. Bathtub

Hotel Steigenberger Treudelberg – Spa

Location:
Hamburg, Germany

Designer:
JOI-Design GmbH

Photographer:
JOI-Design GmbH

Completion date:
2008

JOI-Design's brief for the Hotel Steigenberger Treudelberg was to construct a spa within a resort village that provides an escape from the bustling lifestyle of Hamburg. JOI's solution was the use of natural FF&E materials that relate to the nearby Alster Valley to create an environment that felt secure and holistic for both the nature-based complementary therapies and the more traditional medical treatments. By creating an ambience suitable for leisure and medical holidays, JOI-Design has helped Hotel Steigenberger Treudelberg bring greater value and realise an additional revenue source.

Functional practicalities for delivering alternative treatments such as hydrotherapy and physical rehabilitation are satisfied while retaining the sense of being pampered. Hanseatic chic is expressed in the spa with the use of warm, regional oak and cherry species that, when contrasted with the entry area's crisp cool whites, result in a clean and understated welcome equally suited to a leisurely spa escape or a more formal doctor's check-up. The emphasis between the yin and yang balance of the facility's uses is further underscored through the combination of straight and rounded lines as evidenced in the reception desk and the corridor's horizontal joinery lines offset by the areas' curved pathways and soffits.

1.The graceful corridor
2.The interior ornamentation
3.The flowers and fruit on the bar counter
4.The private room
5.The corridor view from the entrance
6.The bathtub
7.The detail of the washstand

The use of lighting is especially important. Soft lights recessed into the ceilings of treatment rooms cast a warm glow to encourage relaxation, while optional brighter lights are better suited for medical consultations. The round shower with twinkling glass mosaic tiles allows for light reflection and is a touch of sparkle in a design with mostly matte finishes. The natural finishes of the mottled stone floors and woven fibres in the lounge chairs serve as a tangible, textural relief from the technology-fuelled city.

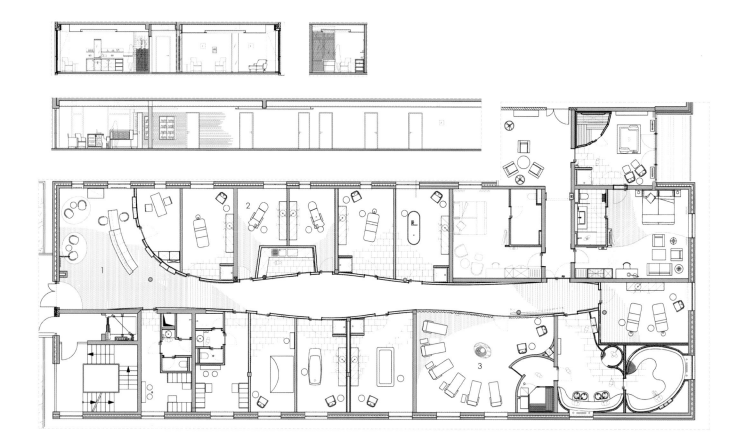

1. Reception
2. Treatment room
3. Lounge

3

6

7

Bergman Beauty Clinics MediSpa

Location:
Amsterdam, The Netherlands

Designer:
Concrete Architectural Associates

Photographer:
Ewout Huibers

Completion date:
2008

Bergman is all about beauty. The best item to express beauty is a mirror and therefore this is the centre theme of the MediSpa. These mirrors are used in the three areas of the MediSpa: the shop, the treatment rooms and the main surgery room. It enlarges the rooms and creates a spacious feeling. Corian is an important material of the interior. Furniture built from corian is seamless. Concrete used this as a metaphor for having a smooth skin.

When guests enter the MediSpa, they are invited to take a seat in the heart of the shop: an island made of corian and smooth white leather surrounded by Bergman's Beauty Products and magazines. Floating white corian cabinets filled with and coloured by Bergman's Beauty products give costumers the opportunity to try the products such as crèmes and make-up.

Inside the four treatment rooms, located on both floors, a spacious and cosy environment is waiting for their guests. Full-length mirrors create the impression of an even more spacious room. White corian cabinets and semi-transparent curtains give the room a smooth and clean appearance.

In the surgery room consumers encounter an open atmosphere. Cabinets of stainless steel, filled with bottles of alcohol give visitors the suggestion of being in a laboratory. A big surgical light is hanging above the white treatment chair.

1.The SPA products are displayed in a clean line
2.There are magazines and TV in the lounge, where the exterior views can be seen
3.The mirrors are the theme of the interior decoration
4.The central island is surrounded by beauty products and magazines
5.The various spa products
6.The luxurious treatment room
7.The benches of the central island

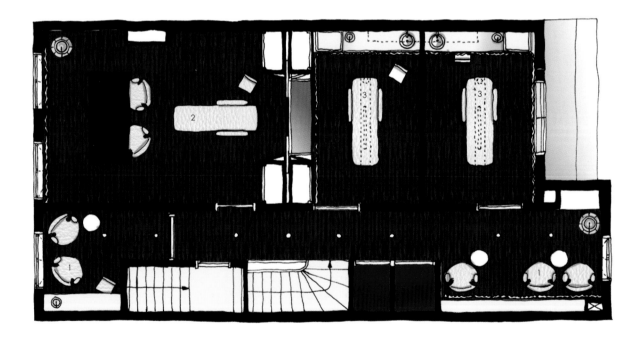

1. Relaxation area
2. VIP treatment room
3. Treatment room

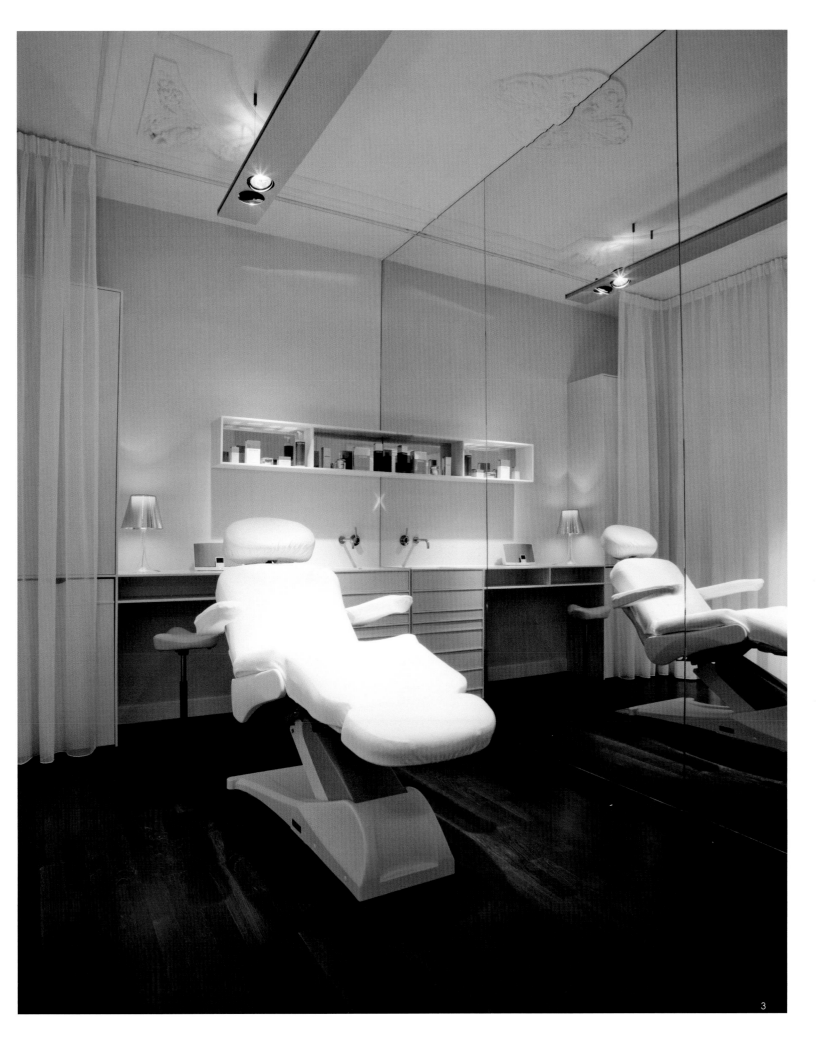

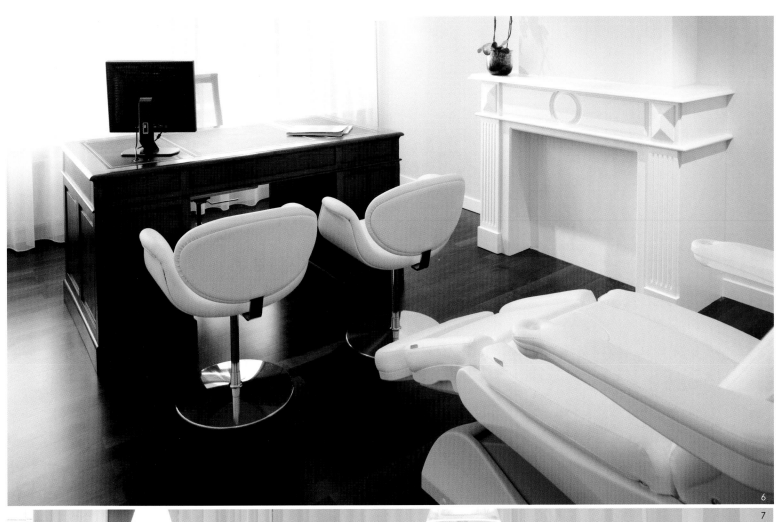

Scandinave Les Bains Vieux-Montréal

Location:
Montréal, Canada

Designer:
Saucier + Perrotte architectes

Photographer:
Marc Cramer

Completion date:
2009

Scandinave Les Bains Vieux-Montréal is an urban spa whose purpose is to provide a thermal therapy experience that engages each of the body's senses. The formal part of the project is derived from the contact between hot and cold – and more specifically, the naturally occurring phenomena associated with these conditions – the design distills the idea of cool glacial forms and the warmness of volcanic rocks.

Upon exiting the dressing room, the visitor is immersed in a unique environment where walls, floors and ceiling are slightly angled according to a notion of interior topography through which visitors may wander. These angles, though subtle, give bathers a perceptual difference from their everyday environs; the awareness of the corporeal relationship with their surroundings is heightened. Just as in a natural landscape, slight undulations in the ground plane create gentle slopes; depressions in the floor level generate basins of water for bathing. At particular moments, volumes emerge from the ground to sculpt interior zones for the sauna and steam bath. Uniting the main space is an undulating wood ceiling that echoes the movements of the floor: walls of white marble mosaic appear to melt at the point of contact with the warm-coloured wood on the ceiling. Heated, cantilevered benches made of black slate offer visitors a warm place to pause in between a hot and cold bathing cycle.

1.The simple and clean interior space
with generous bath pool
2.The design of water screen is unique
3.The steam room
4.The lounge
5.Walking to the bath pool
6.The design style is simple but spacious
7.The dark grey mosaics shows
nobility in coldness

Opalescent glass has been added to admit natural light through the building's existing openings while providing a sense of privacy for the visitors. The light that permeates the bath area glows, adding to the purity of the space and the feeling of tranquility for the bathers while keeping contact with city life. Along the street, a thin cascading layer of water flows on glass surfaces, filtering views so that from the exterior, passersby can see only shadowed silhouettes of the figures within the hot bath. Rounding out the holistic journey is a relaxation room where bathers can relax in rocking chairs or bean-bag lounge chairs.

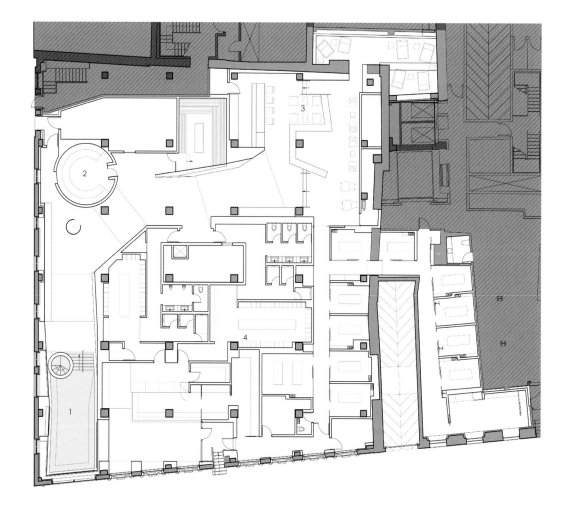

1. Bath pool
2. Stream room
3. Lounge
4. Treatment room

4

5

Cornelia Day Resort

Location:
New York, USA

Designer:
MARKZEFF

Photographer:
Zeff Design

Completion date:
2005

Cornelia Day Resort is located on New York City's famed Fifth Avenue, although it seems worlds away from the hustle and bustle of the busy streets below. Customised care is the core of Cornelia, and the design plan was no different. The designer sets out to create a hideaway, an indulgent day resort where the customer could tailor his own experience, be it holistic or hedonistic, invigorous or relaxing. The space is divided between the 8th and 9th floors of the penthouse in the newly redesigned Ferragamo flagship building. The spa includes both high and low-tech offerings, from endermologie, massage and Romanian-style body treatments to one of New York City's only Watsu pools.

Upon entering the space, guests are greeted in the reception area where cool shimmering celadon tiles and the sound of running water set the tone. The relaxation library, with its plushy carpet, is dimly lit; velvety loungers and comfortable yet structured furniture line the walls, perfect for unwinding before treatments. Guests are encouraged to take a day-long mini vacation. Treatment rooms are tranquil, lined in Venetian plaster and Moroccan tiles. The colour palette is soothing and warm. Following treatments, guests can nosh at the 35-seat café on the roof deck's beautifully landscaped terrace, which is gently shaded by cream canvas umbrellas. The rooftop lounge also boasts private sunbathing areas and shrubbery-

1.The comfortable furniture
2.The detail design is delicate
3.The beauty salon
4.The hairdressing facilities
5.The hairdressing tools
6.Professional treatment facilities

shrouded European soaking baths. Guests can also visit the resort-style boutique, which carries Cornelia products. The spa combines classic elegance with modern amenities, melding the old world with the new.

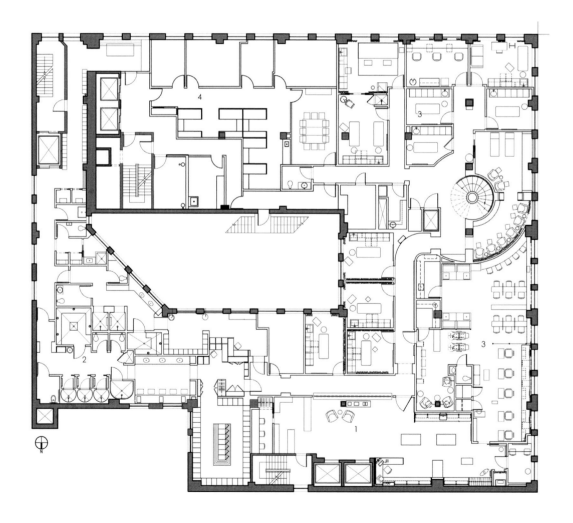

1. Lounge
2. Bathing area
3. Treatment area
4. Office area

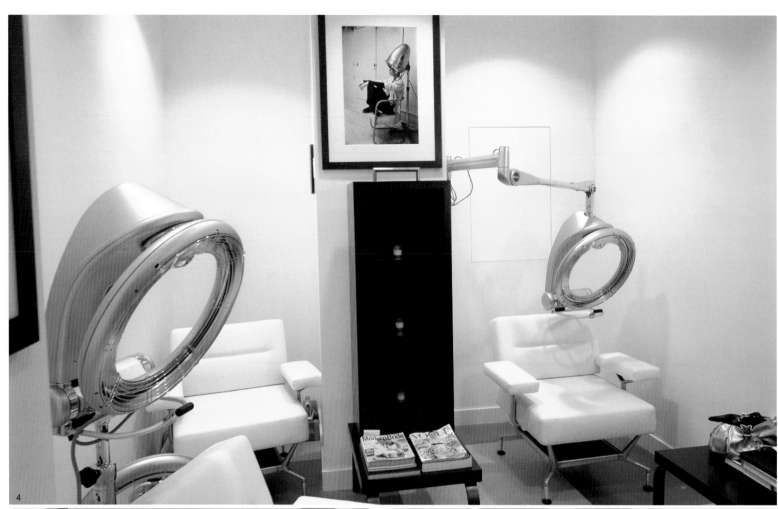

4

5

Oriental Spa Du Parc

Location:
Torino, Italy

Designer:
Stefano Testa, Alessandra Raso/Cliostraat

Photographer:
Franco Lima

Completion date:
2007

The design programme for the Oriental Spa Du Parc seeks within ancient traditions for the ingredients of well-being and personal care which are so precious for today's lifestyle. Since the beginning, the core issue of this interior design was to reminisce the captivating oriental atmosphere while proposing a modern-view interpretation.

The choice of materials is fundamental: the designers wish to find a balance between the traditional references and the contemporary building techniques in order to guarantee a high efficiency both in terms of hygiene and functionality. They wish to define an intriguing set-up on a sensory level in an atmosphere of general cleanliness. The pattern of the petrified fir boards and the cold subsoil light are of key importance for the choice of the colour and texture palette.

The designers organise the correct air-volume for every room, with a careful jigsaw arrangement of the available space. Fluid connections between each space are nevertheless marked thresholds between one activity and the other. The dominating elegant and smooth rosewood, the hard stainless steel, the simply evoked chatoyant bamboo, the opalescent glass and the pitch black of the flooring create a charming and comfortable environment.

1.The light-coloured curtain creates a
fantasy effect
2.The stream and lighting are flowing
down
3.The comfortable couches
4.The fir texture is a natural decoration
5.The space is made up of black
mosaics and sdid wood
6.The simple space in black and white
7.The comfortable treatment room
8.The graceful interior environment

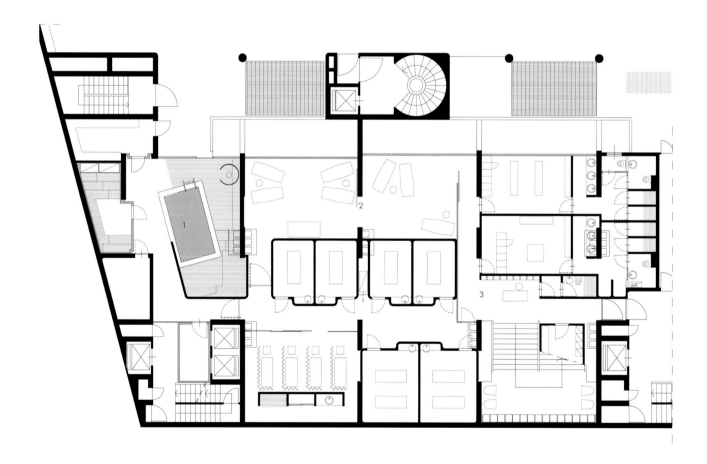

1. Private bathroom
2. Relaxation room
3. Treatment room

3

4

Caudalie Vinothérapie ® Spa

Location:
Elciego, Spain

Designer:
Frank O. Gehry

Photographer:
The Luxury Collection

Completion date:
2007

Caudalie, the French cosmetic niche brand was created in 1995. The owners and founders of Caudalie were fascinated by Elciego and the Rioja wine region of Alava. It was just love at first sight which led them to develop Caudalie Vinothérapie ® Spa, in favour of the new version inspired by the original in Bordeaux. This new version is inspired by the lush colours of the landscape, in the traditions of the area, the identity of Marques de Riscal and the personal signature of the famous architect Frank O. Gehry.

For this wonderful project the designers subtly retained items that are created by the company while integrating Caudalíe draft and landscape of the area. Caudalie Vinothérapie ® Spa has specific and unique treatments in the world, such as honey and wine wrap, exhilarating massage and the Crushed Cabernet Scrub. They are all characterised by the indulgence of the senses, the soothing of the bodies and the regeneration of the soul.

1.The unique exterior form
2.The massage beds are placed in a line
3.There is a relaxation area in the
massage room
4.The red colour reminds people of wine

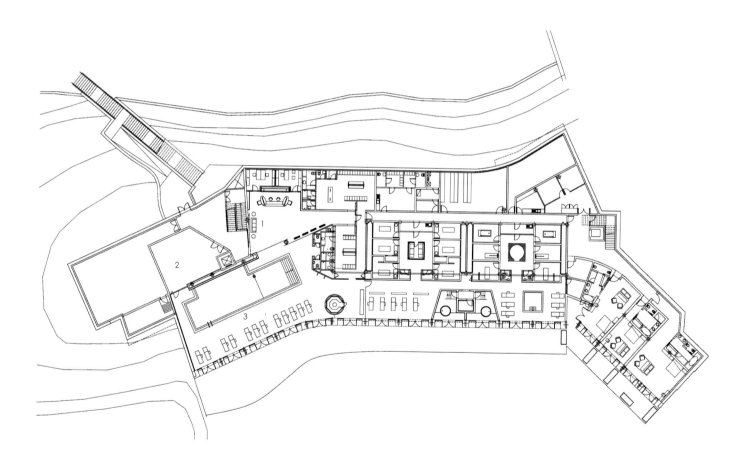

1. Reception
2. Gym
3. Bath pool
4. Spa

3

4

Conti Day Spa

Location:
Terni, Italy

Designer:
Alessio Patalocco

Photographer:
Maurizio Accorroni

Completion date:
2007

The designer cuts a sharp area to have functions with water treatment. In this way, it produces two different ambiences: a wet area and a dry ground. The dry ground is more "public" than the wet one. Seeming kitsch is always a trap for a spa: in a corner where designers search for relaxation away from the day-to-day routine.

The themes of thermal, Turkish baths and saunas are rooted in the past, but today they are decidedly trendy and enjoying an exceptional boom. The designers then renounce the opportunity to create a contemporary architecture for a spa. The whole design is done with elegance and delicateness, leaving people the liberty to imagine their diverse situations in this minute magic world.

It's a work of the designer's imagination, that follow them in these different little places. It is a world balanced between a starry night and the perfumes of an unknown and solitary world where guests can sink into the magic of their whirlpool under a beatiful sky with diamonds.

1.The comfortable massage bed
2.The bathroom with mosaic decoration
3.The unique design creates a unique interior lighting environment
4.The interior space is mysterious and peaceful
5.The ripples flow with the lighting
6.A sense of elegance is created by the combination of red and black
7.The steam room
8.The guests feel as if they were under a starry sky

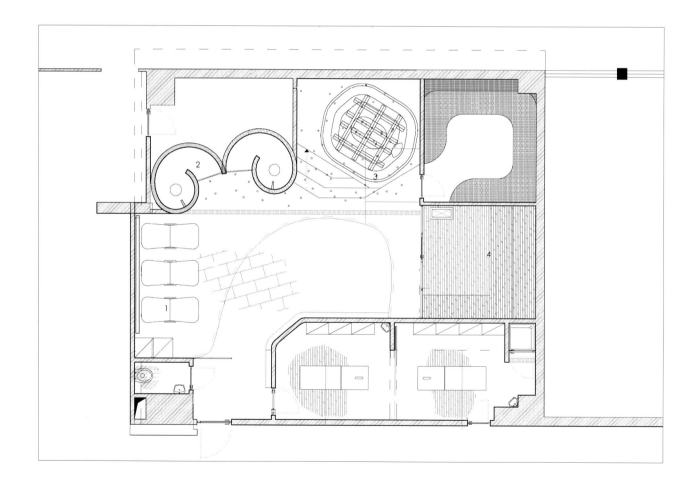

1. Massage bed
2. Shower
3. Bathtub
4. Steam room

3

4

7

8

Lanserhof Health Centre

Location:
Innsbruck, Austria

Designer:
designstudio regina dahmen-ingenhoven

Photographer:
holger knauf

Completion date:
2006

Daylight floods the funnel-shaped health centre through a vast window at the front of the building. Light penetrates the cell-like rooms, which are laid out according to their need for natural light. Doctors' consultation rooms, massage rooms and the lounge are adjacent to the window. Requiring less daylight and situated farther away from the window are reception, pools and treatment rooms. Offices and storerooms are at the rear. The reception area, at the heart of the facility, leads directly to the main lounge. A large, round, bright-blue sofa fosters communication among the guests, whose gaze is drawn to the view of the mountains through the glass frontage. A photo of the same panoramic view covers a 50-metre-long translucent wall that runs parallel to the glazed façade, separating massage and consultation rooms from circulation areas. Entering one of the doors in the wall with the photo, the visitor sees an identical mountain vista, but now through the window. The designers brought nature into the space to establish harmony between outdoors and indoors.

Wet areas behind the reception zone include pools, showers and spas. Reflecting the theme of water, they are clad in bisazza mosaic tiles in various shades of blue. The tiled surfaces mirror the motif of circular holes – seen in the acoustic ceilings, for example – that is repeated in every room, making a purely functional necessity into

1.The interior space is clean and simple
2.Guests can enjoy the natural view through the windows
3.The blue mosaics bring a fresh sense of ocean
4.In the relaxation area, the French window connects the interior and exterior space
5.The comfortable wonderland feels like a home
6.The relatively independent reception
7.The private treatment room

part of the design. These "polka dots" bring oxygen bubbles to mind.

Circles also appear in some of the treatment rooms, but as yellow openings of various sizes in the walls, which are lit from within. Built-in lighting is an important design device at Lanserhof, where all illumination is indirect. Pure white light or coloured light streams out of niches, slits and holes, creating a serene atmosphere. The only conventional lamps to be seen are flush-mounted spots in the acoustic ceilings. All furniture in the medical therapeutic centre was purpose-designed by the dahmen-ingenhoven team.

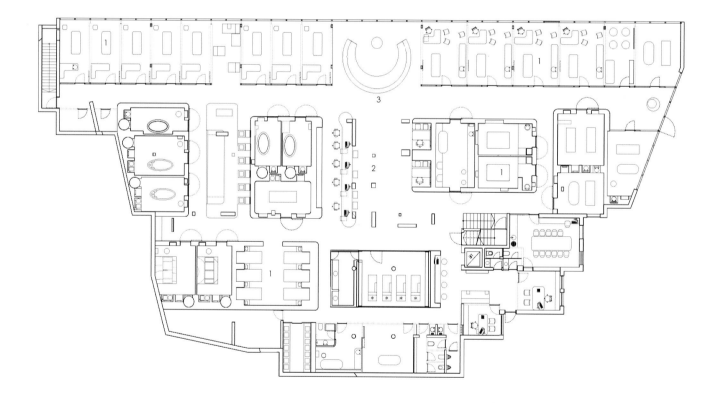

1. Treatment room
2. Reception
3. Lounge

Bathhouse Spa

Location:
Las Vegas, USA

Designer:
Guillermo Garita, Alex Grossmann

Photographer:
Andrew Bordwin Studio, Inc

Completion date:
2006

The concept of Bathhouse draws from the traditional Roman spa experience – baths and communal services – in a very private manner. A meditative space anchored by very public experiences – plunge pools, soaking tubs, steam and sauna rooms, open rainfalls, Bathhouse reveals itself in small moments, creating the feeling of privacy in a very open environment. The energy of Vegas disappears and a contemplative space appears, quiet and tranquil, in which guests can find balance in the midst of this fabled desert.

The glass and stone hideaway houses several treatment rooms and lounges designed to offer guests a multitude of the latest in treatments and products. The house lines – Infuse, Immerse and Submerge – are designed to offer guests the opportunity to recreate their own experiences, whether they have ten minutes (Infuse), one hour (Immerse) or three hours (Submerge).

1.Walking into the bath area
2.The pool is decorated with pebbles
3.The comfortable bath environment
4.The products area
5.The lighting design of the corridor
6.The detail design is humane
7.The lounge next to the corridor

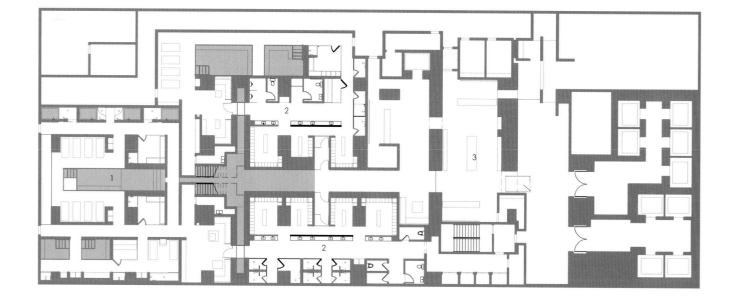

1. Treatment room
2. Dressing room
3. Bath pool

3

4

Mizu Spa

Location:
San Francisco, USA

Designer:
Stanley Saitowitz/Natoma Architects Inc.

Photographer:
Cesar Rubio

Completion date:
2007

Mizu is water, which Mizu Spa embodies. The atmosphere is a tranquil stream. At the centre is a river of rock, around which the communal therapy barge floats in space. The walls are draped in shimmering mesh creating light and fluid edges. The horizontal surfaces of floor and ceiling are black. Everything else is pure and white. One will feel peaceful and quiet in this white and black space.

There are also some specially designed sittings in the space, such as the pure white comfortable sofas, where one can lie on the soft back cushion when having the foot spa , or reading newspapers, magazines. Besides, there are some waiting chairs beside the spa area. There are many built-in wardrobes in the walls in order to store the Bath Linen.

Mizu Spa is a place for pampering, rejuvinating and transforming. Treatments include facials, massage and nails. The central object is a prosthetic throne to sit on. Soft pads pamper the body. Arms rest, hands support, feet soak, and the provider glides around on stools.

Behind the communal therapy area are private rooms for facials and massage. In this place, the white and black colour tone was continued by the designers, and besides, there is a line of cobblestone on each bed which was covered by some pure white towels. In the bathroom, below the sinks, rocks again appear as water.

1.The pure white comfortable sofas
for foot spa
2.The detail design of the massage bed
3.A river of black pebbles can be
seen from the entrance
4.The interior design applies black
and white palette

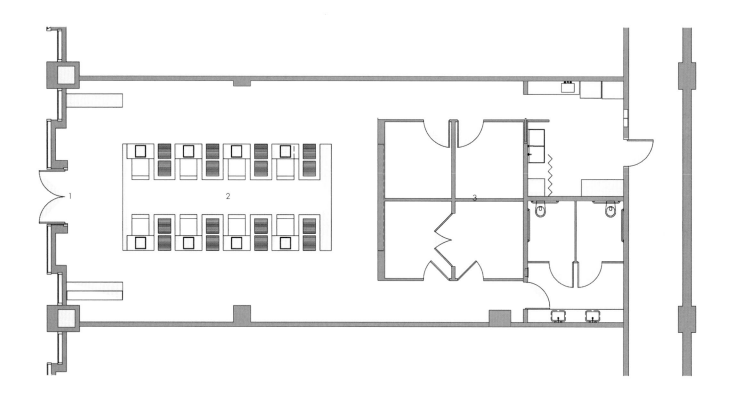

1. Entrance
2. Treatment area
3. Private treatment room

Kanebo Sensai Select Spa

Location:
Interlaken, Switzerland

Designer:
CURIOSITY

Photographer:
NACASA & PARTNERS

Completion date:
2009

Kanebo Sensai Select Spa is a haven of Japanese healing and beauty traditions offering the luxurious infusion of Koishimaru Silk, a precious variety from Japan known as the "silk of silks". Uniting the hidden power of Koishimaru Silk and the Japanese hot spring into spa treatments for the first time, the spa promises the ultimate beauty and reinvigorated spirit.

The Sensai experience is a journey through sequences of sensorial encounters. The Japanese esthetic is a subtle balance of simplicity created from complexity. Sensai is a high prestige cosmetic brand of Kanebo which is mainly developed in Europe. The design of the space is based on the lining of floating layers of Koishimaru silk, a core value of the Sensai brand. The design leads visitors from the dark corridor of the hotel past the silk layers to a circular waiting room. The waiting room in the centre of the space is designed as a "cocoon", an oasis of tranquility surrounded by serene light. The everyday life gives way to a different dimension. The interior design leads to an unexplored sense of relaxation and well-being. Treatment rooms have warm wooden walls and timber shelves linked to the ceiling by metal poles. A lighting wall is created with layers of interlaced strings of fabric. Reflection, refraction, distortion, light and shadow create a play for the senses, while space, material and light fuse into immateriality, where body and mind tune into harmony.

1.The arc-shaped screen separates a
semi-private space
2.The silk screen
3.The design is in Japanese style
4.The private treatment room

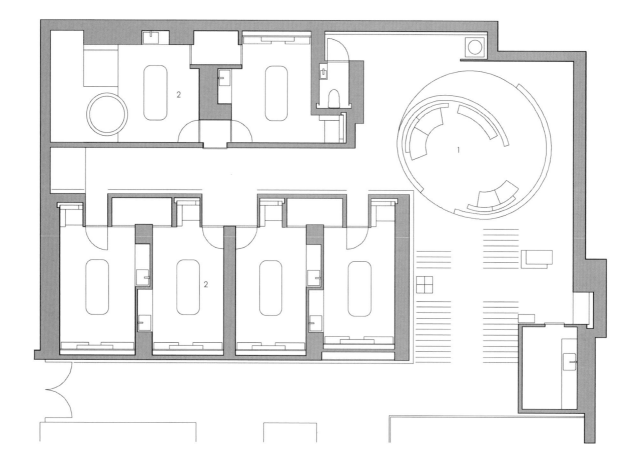

1. Reception
2. Treatment room

3

4

Hillside City Club

Location:
Istanbul, Turkey

Designer:
GAD & Gokhan Avcioglu

Photographer:
Ozlem Avcioglu

Completion date:
2008

Hillside City Club is located in Istanbul's Istinye Park mall complex, a lively public destination where people may satisfy their demands for high-quality goods and services. Therefore, the Hillside City Club responded to a desire already present given the nature the area. This would serve as a basis for inspiration, and reinforced the value of this project. The Hillside City Club is a total of 6,000 square metres, and provides a number of services to its 12,000 members, including a gym complete with cardio & studio classes, squash, racquetball, tennis, & basketball courts, and a variety of group exercises accompanied by a certified expert trainer. Also, Hillside City Club is the location of Turkey's first and largest "SPA in SANDA" chain.

Architecturally, the programmatic organisation of the complex is arranged around a number of "social nodes", or destinations, which are intended as areas for social mixing and interaction. Additionally, the architect's design objective was to create varying experiences with spatial volumes throughout the complex. The combination of these "social nodes" and "spatial volumes" offers an architecturally diverse environment, and serves to supplement the various activities and services taking place at Hillside.

Typically, one will approach Hillside City Club and enter by lifts accessed from the mall below. A reception desk is located as one

1.The wall decoration is unique
2.It has a natural feeling to use woods and pebbles as decoration
3.The comfortable and clean interior space
4.The treatment room

arrives from the lifts, and the visitors are dispatched to one of the following nodes: the spa, locker rooms, and other support spaces including a hair salon, book shop, organic nutrition shop, restaurant & café. Locker rooms are provided for the users, and offer a number of accessory functions including lockers, showers, restrooms, resting areas, steam rooms, saunas, and cold shock showers. There are two pools in the club, both exterior and interior, totaling 1,000 square metres. One pool is located adjacent to the locker rooms, and a sunbathing terrace is located above the closed pool providing easy access to the terrace.

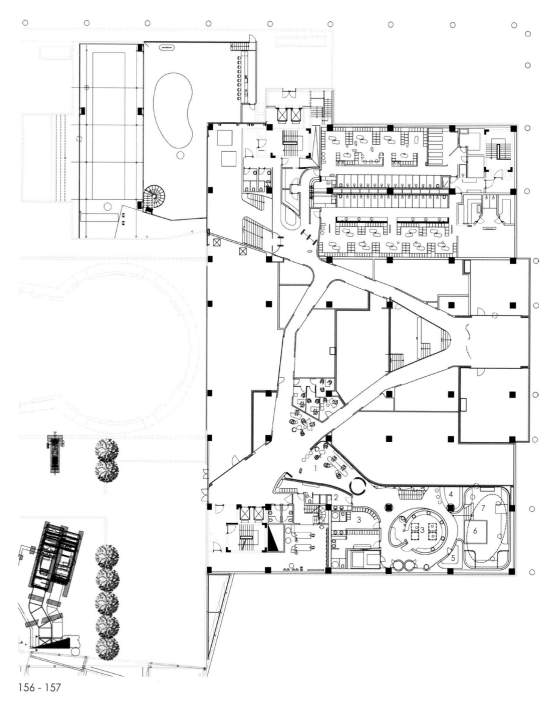

1. Entrance
2. Staff locker
3. Locker room
4. Bar
5. Steam room
6. Jacuzz
7. Resting room

Aveda + Xenses Lifestyle Spa & Salon

Location:
Hong Kong, China

Designer:
ALEXCHOI design & Partners

Photographer:
Rage Wan

Completion date:
2007

Aveda + Xenses Lifestyle Spa & Salon is located in Causeway Bay, at an abandoned "dungeon"-like basement with an area of 10,000 square feet. With the synergy of this abandoned basement and silence, the roar of the city is muted and composes a sweet and intimate sound.

Chemistry happened when two spas co-exist in the same area but serve different visitors. Aveda focuses on adolescents while Xenses serves the maturity. Competition gives way to deep sense of harmony since Aveda and Xense share the same concept – relaxation and comfort. It is quite annoying that many columns stand inside the basement. To harmonise the atmosphere, and make it a place to peace and ease of mind, those columns are concealed by treatment room which in turn creates maze-like layout and generate a sense of exploration and intimacy. Then the concealed light trough creates cosiness. The consistent use of shaded brownish colour matches with the floral arrangement in Aveda, and the use of sustainable bamboo matches with the feature "tri-colour" geometric sand stone in Xenses. The two combinations together bring out the aim of recycle and also reinforce the theme of nature.

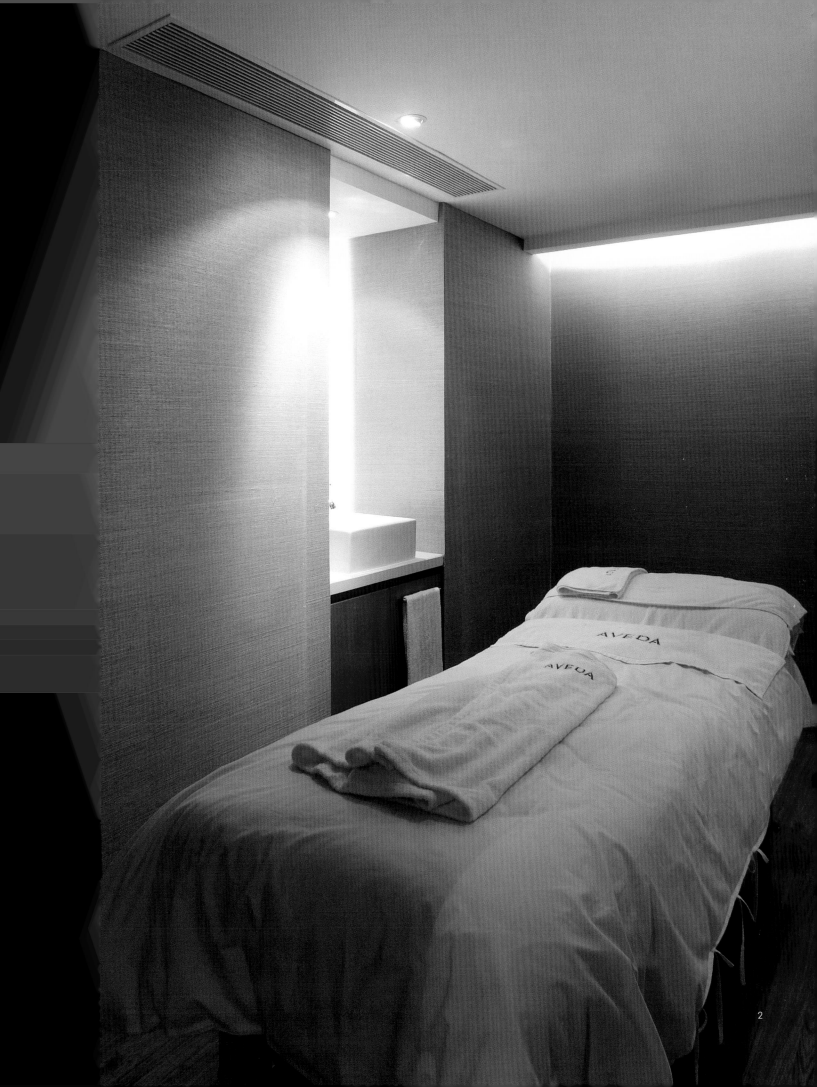

1.The reception of Xenses
2.In the clean treatment room, the washstand can be hidden behind the sliding door
3.The staircase
4.The foot spa area
5.The private treatment room
6.The flower arrangement is used as a decoration of the washstand
7.The hairdressing salon
8.The simple glass screen

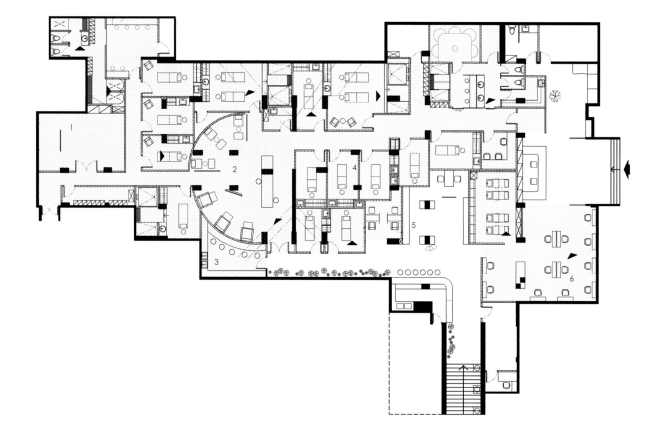

1. Meditation room
2. Relaxation area
3. Staff room
4. Treatment room
5. Reception
6. Salon

3

4

5

6

M One Spa

Location:
Taipei, China

Designer:
Tange Associates

Completion date:
2009

M One Spa is located on a quiet side street of the trendy, high-end area of Renai Road in Taipei. M One Spa's aim is to appeal to those customers who go to spas frequently. When those customers are in the city, M One Spa provides the quality and luxury they would otherwise receive only from a global class destination spa.

As guests approach the entrance, they are intrigued by the large, red column at the corner of the building. Tables and chairs on the terrace indicate the trendy M One Café, but it is not until inside that guests realise the presence of a spa. A doorman greets guests and ushers them to the spa's lower level. A glass partition featuring cascading water separates the interior and outside terraces. The space is decorated with soothing dark grey quartz, black marble and moabi wood. The natural materials and healing music are the first introduction to a complete relaxation experience.

As guests descend the steps to the treatment rooms, the tranquil atmosphere deepens. The high gloss sheen of black marble, black glass and black stainless steel, as well as mirrors create a sense of limitless space. At the centre of the lower level the guest lounge evokes the image of a flame with its red silk curtains. Oversized furniture upholstered in golden silk fabric invites guests to savour the moments of leisure.

1.The lobby
2.The interior landscape enhances
the peaceful atmosphere
3.The detail design of the washstand
4.The treatment room
5.The treatment room
6.The treatment room
7.The treatment room

Guests proceed through a dimly lit corridor as if in a walking meditation, leaving the mundane behind and entering the peaceful and sensuous world of one of the 15 private treatment rooms. The corridor terminates in red silk curtains, evoking the same image of a flame as the guest lounge. Each treatment room contains its own dressing area, toilet and shower room that looks out onto a private bamboo garden. The high level of privacy allows guests to surrender fully to the spa experience.

1. Staff office
2. Massage room
3. Parking
4. Lounge
5. Reception

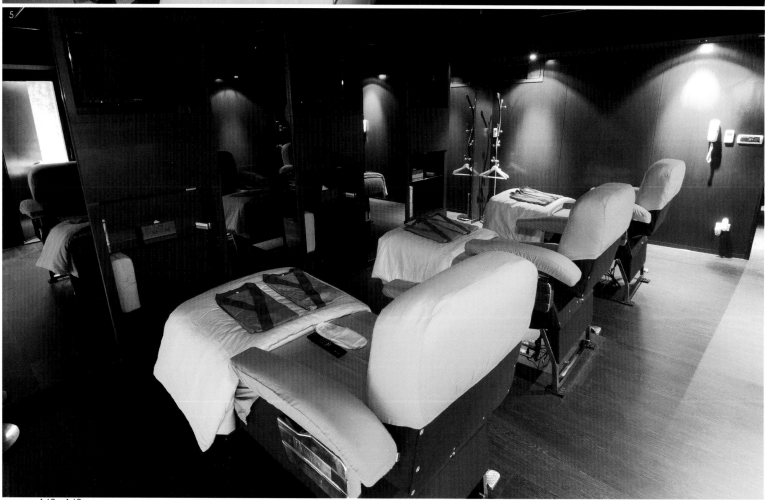

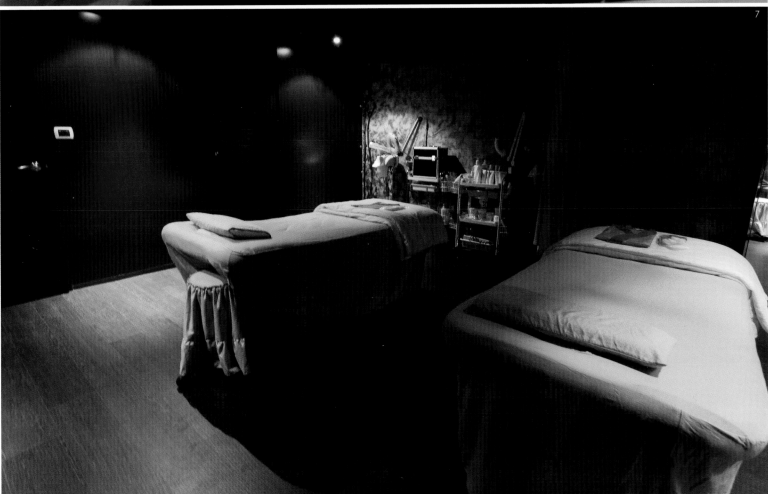

Spa Gardish

Location:
Yokohama, Japan

Designer:
ZNEM

Photographer:
Masaya Yoshimura

Completion date:
2007

Spa Gardish is a day's spa institution added to the suburban model sports club. You can use a spa alone. It is an institution consisting of a bathhouse and an outdoor bath of the each man and woman, bedrock bath, the warm bath zone for families of the man and woman joint ownership, a healing corner, rest corner (reflexology, body, a Thai ancient rite, a head spa) and the private room where a massage is caught and a restaurant.

As for Spa Gardish, it is difficult to secure space of the opening so that there is it in a shopping centre. Therefore the architect directed a feeling of opening by designing half of the positions of the bathhouse part in "an outdoor bath" even if it had the eaves. The architect takes in a lot of Nipponian elements and directs it so that it is felt air of four seasons for the five senses by the natural and anonymous design. The architect wants you to pay your attention to indirect lighting in particular and indirect sound. The art object is lighted in illumination. The bamboo carries the good wishes, and the LED light flashing on and off automatically in a motif lights up the space softly. A sound of water drips down from the waterfall where the architect piles up a pebble at the outdoor bath, and is made to intercept the noise from the outside. The placement of the speaker in the institution is devised, too. The designer plans the interesting indirect sound by using

1.The entrance to the spa
2.Both the application of materials and interior decoration are close to nature
3.The Japanese style is simple but graceful
4.The warm interior lighting
5.The indoor shower room
6.The exterior part enables the guests to get close to nature
7.There are several interior bath pools

a swing speaker. Plants are to create a good environment and people here can enjoy a delicious meal. People who visited it thoroughly can enjoy the cosiness and can be relaxed heartily.

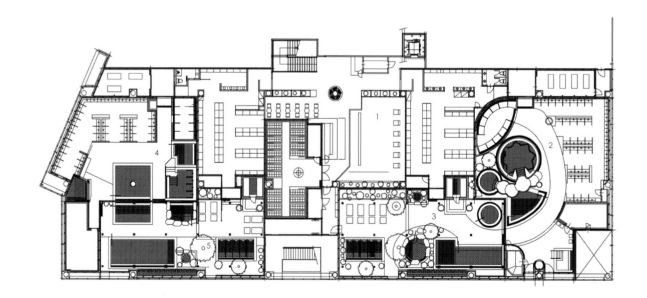

1. Lobby
2. Women's spa
3. Outdoor women's spa
4. Men's spa
5. Outdoor men's spa

6

7

Hard Rock Spa

Location:
Las Vegas, USA

Designer:
MARKZEFF

Photographer:
Eric Laignel

Completion date:
2010

The designer's mission was to create a new luxury spa and salon for guests to enjoy at the Las Vegas Hotel. When designing the spa, the designer pulled inspiration from the famous art nouveau spa in Budapest and a touch of rock, n' roll details. The 6.2-million-dollar, 35,000-square-foot spa is the first to offer a communal hot tub the size of a swimming pool with lounging rooms and surrounding day bed alcoves. Each lounging room has its own steam room with fireplaces and library. The pool area is adorned with vivid blue and green tiles with black and metal detailing, ceilings are tiled with Terracotta and the wet areas have classic white with brown and grey mosaic tiled floors. The 21 treatment rooms have a silver/grey-patterned wallpaper with silver and brown flooring. The spa space commands an immediate feeling of grand opulence with the dramatic barrel vaulted tiled ceilings, bronze furniture and immense detailing on every surface. The new spa provides guests with the ability to enjoy the spa 24/7 and offers additional amenities including: an entertainment area for small parties, a private studio for pole dancing lessons, a fitness centre and the salon. When creating the look of the new salon, the designer chose to incorporate an industrial look with a clean and pure style. Rough limed oak wood floors highlight the pure white counter and wall surfaces of the salon, giving it a subtle glow. Brightly coloured oil paintings by a local artist give a pop of colour to the neutral palette and the retail area in the front gives a masculine contrast with matt black steal with antiqued brass nail head details.

1.The swimming pool
2.The blue and green tiles are decorated with metal patterns
3.The beauty salon has a simple industry style
4.Each lounging room has its own steam room with fireplaces and library
5.The retail area in the front gives a masculine contrast with matt black steal with antiqued brass nail head details
6.The treatment room has a full set of facilities
7.Bright sunlight can be enjoyed in the beauty salon

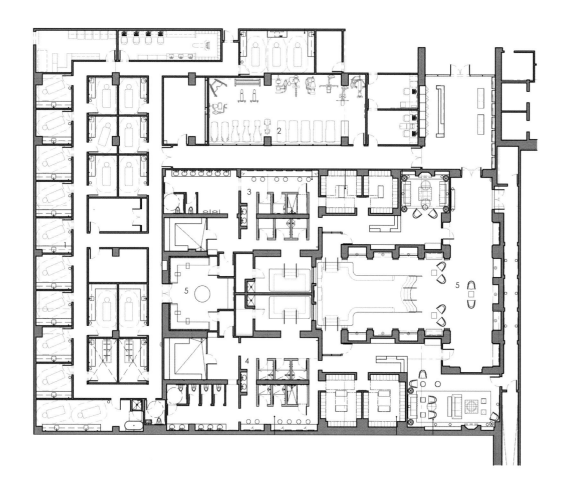

1. Treatment room
2. Gym
3. Men's spa
4. Women's spa
5. Lounge

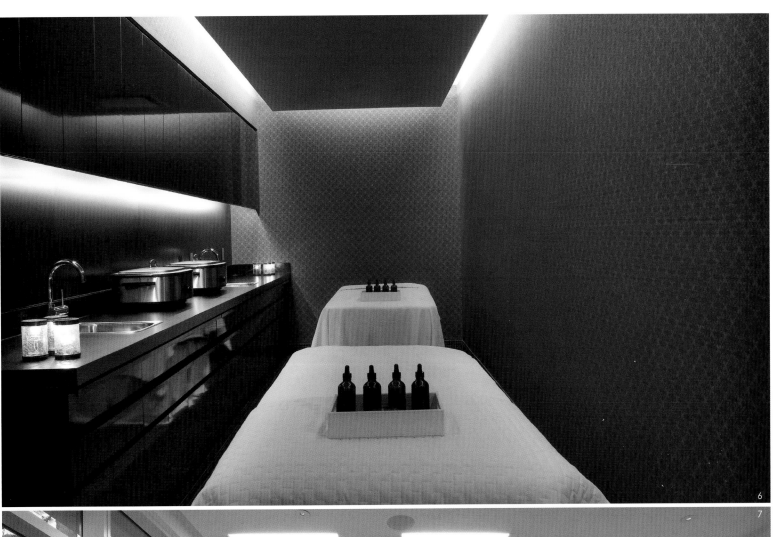

6

7

Hypnotique Spa

Location:
Milan, Italy

Designer:
Simone Micheli

Photographer:
Simone Micheli Architectural Hero

Completion date:
2009

Hypnotique Spa, the installation with an emotional and vital mood, has become an attractive centre for the sensorial wakening, as a relaxing oasis made by conceptual contaminations, where metropolitan man can put in stand-by urban frantic paces to cuddle his soul and spend time to rediscover the pleasure of getting exited. In the words of Architect Micheli, there is the crux of the expositive performance: "In this place man has been collocated in the middle with his senses and stimulated with shapes, lights and colours, to be carried away in a dimension that is placed between immanence and transcendence, between fantasy and reality. Every element has been thought to touch his heart, to excite him, to sweetly caress him with a light breeze of joy and lightness. In this way is expressed a new conception of luxury, tied together an intimacy of sensations."

The spa offers a suggestive path with a high perceptive stimulation with massaging water jets, perfumes, lights and colours, whereas a soft and pure creaminess of the ceiling and the fluid walls create a dreaming and wrapping atmosphere. From this creamy background emerge the dividing walls and the compounding elements which, with their warm and bright colours, become an extraordinary attraction source for the eyes, completing a surreal scenery where we could immerge soul and body. An "other" place

1.The design is bright and lively
2.In this place one can enjoy himself to his heart's content, stimulated by the shapes, lights and colours, and carried away in a dimension between fantasy and reality
3.The soft and pure creaminess of the ceiling and the fluid walls create a dreaming atmosphere
4.The interior design is surprising
5.The considerate detail design

where architecture, sensoriality and wellness melt together gives life to a new improbable dimension, all to perceive. The fluidity of this place has aimed to become lifeblood of the regenerating power, able to reactivate visitors' sensoriality who came back to listen and listen to themselves again. In a reality where the unceasing frenzy exasperates the sense of uncertainty of everyone, excessively multiplying the possible ways and resetting the ground friction, the only path to follow is that of our dreams.

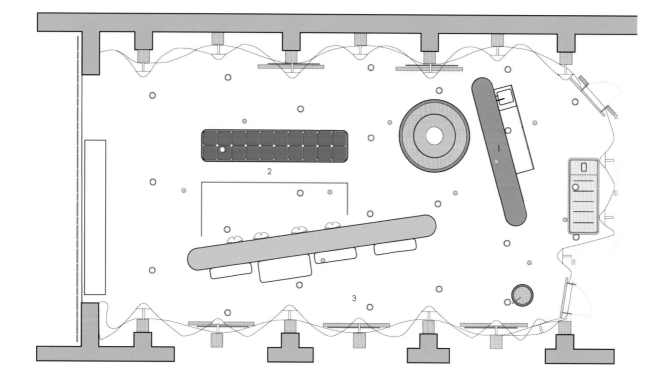

1. Reception
2. Bath area
3. Massage area

Mars The Salon Spa Boutique

Location:
Tokyo, Japan

Designer:
CURIOSITY

Photographer:
NACASA & PARTNERS

Completion date:
2008

"Mars The Salon Spa Boutique", situated in Aoyama, has extended into a new space with a spa boutique. Following their success with the nail salon Mars, CURIOSITY has also designed this spa. While keeping the same spatial identity, the more dramatic spa contrasts nicely with the nail salon's bright and airy feel. The space is designed with a rhythm of vertical light and shadow strokes that creates a visual tempo. They are reminiscent of "Torii", the gates to a shrine marking the division between the physical and the mental worlds.

The entrance of the spa includes a shop area. The vertical element is also used to house the displays suspended from the ceiling. Following the dramatically-lit corridor, a peaceful and relaxing space welcomes the customer for consulting before and after treatment. Two long treatment rooms run alongside the corridor. The all-in-one individual rooms include treatment beds, an original nail treatment sofa with integrated footbath. The different zones inside the rooms are separated by a series of vertical wood louvres.

1.The flower arrangement embellishes
the comfortable space
2.The treatment room
3.Each corner has a delicate decoration
4.The vertical boards and horizontal
glass bring a unique vision
5.The vertical light-and-shadow design
6.The peaceful and relaxing area

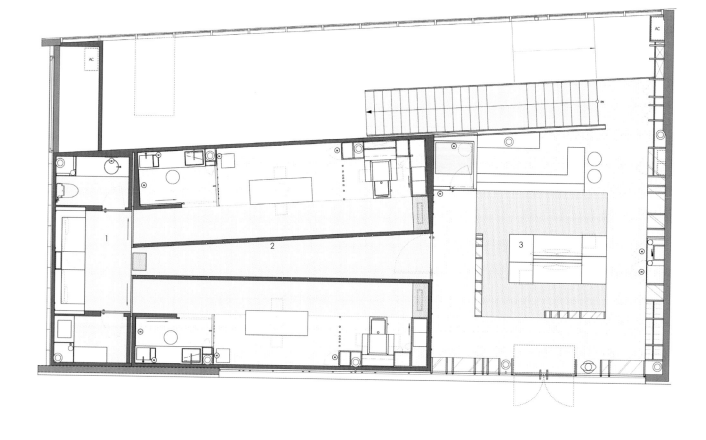

1. Staff area
2. Treatment area
3. Lounge

Mission Hills Spa – Spring Valley

Location:
Shenzhen, China

Designer:
Joey Ho/Joey Ho Design Ltd.

Photographer:
Ray Lau

Completion date:
2006

The Spring Valley provides a luxurious backdrop for spa activities. It also amplifies the sensual qualities that complement the whole victual of going to a spa. The spa is designed to blend into the harmonious space where peace meets light.

Spatial arrangement based on pavilions and linkage walkway is adopted for the design to create a "journey" where visitors have to go through a decompression zone to prepare oneself for the upcoming spa experience. The spa design is to invoke the five senses and has to be sensitively orchestrated to heighten one's experience. As one enters this exotically oriental and unique establishment, the reflecting pool with the pavilion-like floating spa café and entrance pavilion fringed by aromatic indigenous trees and plants engage one's serves of sight, sound and smell. The water fountain set behind the reception area gurgles harmoniously to a sort of natural musical arrangement.

Natural soft light pervades the facilities through diaphanous window treatments, illuminating the interiors with a sense of spaciousness and ethereal comfort. It is believed that nature can greatly enrich one's perception and sympathy for beauty. Therefore spa treatment rooms are purposefully geared towards the meditative garden and water features.

1.The guests prepare themselves for the "journey" before the spa
2.The lighting design makes the interior space comfortable and peaceful
3.The delicate night scene
4.The public treatment room
5.The delicate wall decoration in the treatment room
6.One can enjoy natural atmosphere in the treatment room
7.The bathtub and massage bed in the private treatment room
8.The detail design is unique

The perception of space exudes freedom, yet warmth and intimacy are not far off. Elements are incorporated into this creation solely designed to inspire changes of mood. Influenced by yin-yang oriental beliefs, the spa is about creating an environment of peaceful equilibrium.

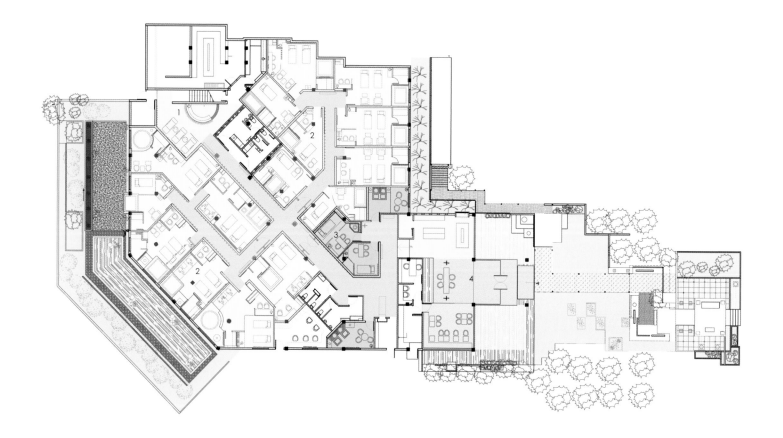

1. Relaxation room
2. Treatment room
3. Products area
4. Reception

3

4

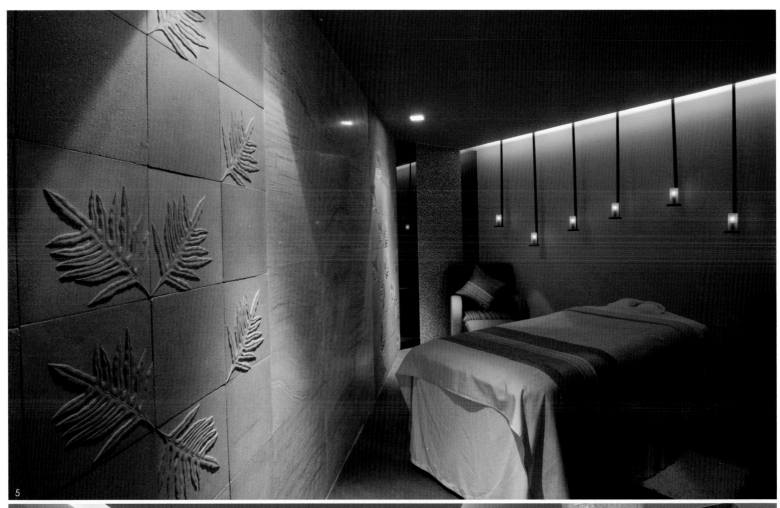

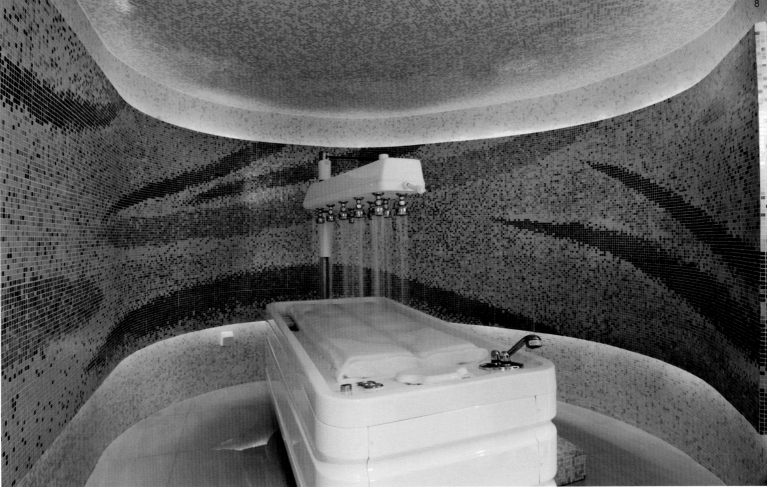

Spa by MTM Shanghai

Location:
Shanghai, China

Designer:
Patrick Leung

Photographer:
Bao Shi Wang/PAL Design Consultants
Ltd.

Completion date:
2008

A principal of Minimalism Aesthetic, the space design emphasises on extreme leisure and comfort, providing an experience of a journey from body relaxation to soul touch. This brand spa by MTM achieved the successful business in Hong Kong's first branch. The booming development of spa business has extended to Mainland China. Thus the retail design inspiring a contemporary natural artistic approach is the extension of the brand concept into a new branch in Shanghai.

The facility is located on the whole floor with a total area of 2,000 square metres. Space is invisible, integrated with the function of spa through the natural elements, and creates a sense of chic, comfort and silence. Concerning the spread of Line, curved wood stripes extend from main lobby to every spa treatment room. An arc ceiling or stripe partition enhances the beauty of peace. Prime material wood with curved shape expresses a unique architectural form in a perfect art craft.

After departure from the lift lobby, there is a reception table made of black glass and marble contrasting with the white bright lobby. To produce a welcoming and pleasant environment, seating layout sets beside at the corner of the green wall. A quiet moment is well issued by simple woodcarving art. White is the main colour tone for pureness, freshness and nature ingenuity match with green as

1. The natural elements are used in interior decoration
2. The curved wood line extends from the lobby to every treatment room
3. The quiet treatment room
4. The reception in black marble contrasts with the white lobby
5. The soft and mysterious lighting design
6. The treatment room
7. The benches in the corridor

the cheerful touch tone. Moreover, subtle application of lighting provides an attentively consideration from bright lobby switching dim light to the corridor for its serene refinement. The curved dim pathway with two-side wood stripe partitions imagines that a client desires the placid mood.

There are thirteen single and two dual treatment rooms giving privacy for guests with real sensation. Every room provides sanitary ware, while some special rooms provide Jacuzzi facilities. With soft colour scheme, simple screen adds to the space more cleanliness and harmony. The dedicate details serve guests for the meticulous spa enjoyment.

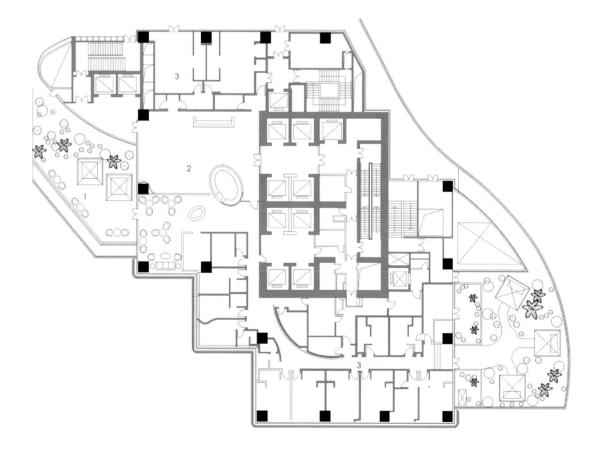

1. Relaxation area
2. Reception
3. Treatment room

6

7

The World's First Underwater Spa

Location:
Maldives

Designer:
Richard Hywel Evans Architecture &
Design Ltd.

Completion date:
2009

The underwater spa, which forms part of the luxury Huvafen Fushi Resort in the Maldives, comprises two treatment rooms and a separate relaxation area with mind-blowing views under the Indian Ocean. The $180,000 redesign of the interior creates the boldest and most sensory appealing spa in the world.

Guests enter the underwater spa along a passageway lit with colour-changing lights in the ceiling to enhance the overall sensory experience. Once inside, reconfigurable sliding walls allow the space to be opened up to make the most of the spectacular views or closed to create a more intimate space for treatments. The transformation also includes lifting the interior wall colour from a light wood to a double curvature organic form, installing a stretch Barisol ceiling and replicating the sea floor by laying blue resin-bonded pebble tiles under the foot.

1.Fishes are swimming before your eyes
2.The spa entrance on the ground
3.The interior design resembles the
underwater view
4.It feels like an underwater palace
5.Schools of fish are swimming near
the windows
6.Every fish can be seen clearly
7.The use of glass makes the spa a
crystal palace

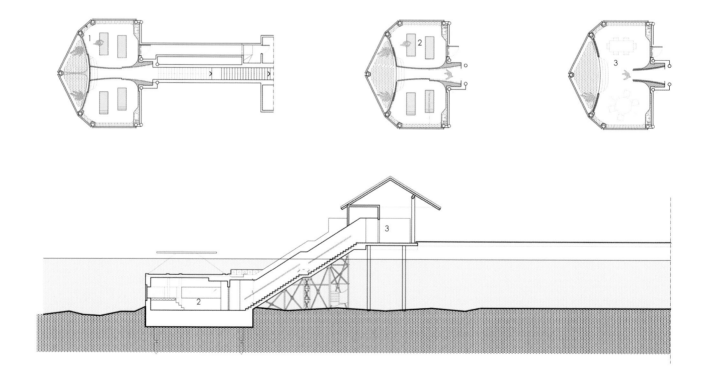

1. Relaxation area
2. Treatment room
3. Reception

Shinsegae Centum City Spaland

Location:
Busan, Korea

Designer:
Hashimoto Yukio Design Studio Inc.

Photographer:
Nacasa and Partners Inc.

Completion date:
2009

This spa is in the commercial complex, Shinsegae Centum City. Shinsegae, one of the three biggest Korean department stores, created the biggest scale shopping complex in Asia, and Spaland is inside the complex. The designers achieve to create extraordinary resort space with the theme of "Relax & Enjoy" using water, light and natural materials to symbolise the richness of the nature of Busan.

Spaland consists of two floors. The ground-floor lobby is a dynamic space with wooden columns, pendants, indirect lighting and flowing water from the ceiling. Guests receive spa-wear and head to the bath area through each locker rooms. The bath area has natural hot spring bath, and for ladies, there are outside hot spring also. Making the most of its high ceiling, they used curved lines and curved surfaces.

Guests can enjoy co-ed area if they go through the atrium after changing their clothes to spa-wear. Outside the footbath has circle-shape luminous ceilings, which looks as if the object is continuously floating. Jjimjilbang area has water basin and lantern So guests would feel as if they are in a different country resort. Jjimjilbang has twelve kinds of rooms. "Hanjungmak" has indirect lighting to create a modern feeling. "Rock salt room" is full of piled-up bricks of rock salt and lighting behind. Guests can also enjoy in other rooms with various characters and effects.

1.The wide interior corridor
2.The bath pool
3.The warm lighting design provides
an exotic feeling
4."Rock salt room"
5.Here guests can enjoy full relaxation
6.The circular bath pool
7.The graceful interior environment

On the first floor, there are a café, a restaurant, a VIP room, a relaxation room, a DVD room, a business centre, a fitness studio and an esthetic-salon room. Guests can experience dining, watching TV at the relaxation room, having esthetic massage, and lots of other relaxation functions after they enjoy the bath and Jjimjilbang.

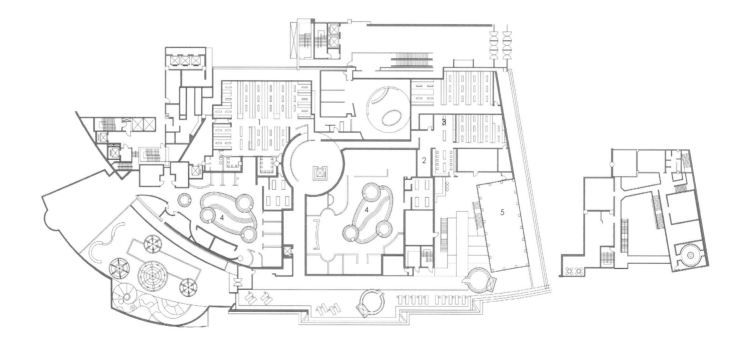

1. Female dressing room
2. Male dressing room
3. Hair salon
4. Bath pool
5. Lounge

6

7

MAVIDA Balance Spa

Location:
Salzburg, Austria

Designer:
Niki Szilagyi, Evi Märklstetter

Photographer:
Niki Szilagyi

Completion date:
2008

The holistic concept behind the MAVIDA Balance Spa aims to create a sense of "flowing privacy", a homogenous space that always places the individual at the centre. Located in the splendid mountain landscape near Austria's Lake Zell and affording views of snowcapped Alpine peaks, the MAVIDA is the destination for wellness and recuperation. Its inviting understated modern design not only generates an atmosphere of relaxing elegance, but is sensitively implemented to promote inner balance.

The real peace takes place in the stunning state-of-the-art spa. Here massive blocks of slate create a dramatic backdrop for ultimate relaxation in a wide array of treatments and services: recharge in one of many saunas, relax in the floatation, rejuvenate in a "blue box" with special light and sound techniques, or refresh near the new 25-metre-long outdoor pool. Then they can walk to the resort's private lakeside beach, watch the sunset over the glassy water, and experience a sublime natural calm.

1.The lounge
2.The comfortable chairs and tables
generate hpme-like warmth
3.The bath pool
4.The delicate hall
5.The bath pool
6.The warm relaxation area
7.The treatment room provides
courteous service

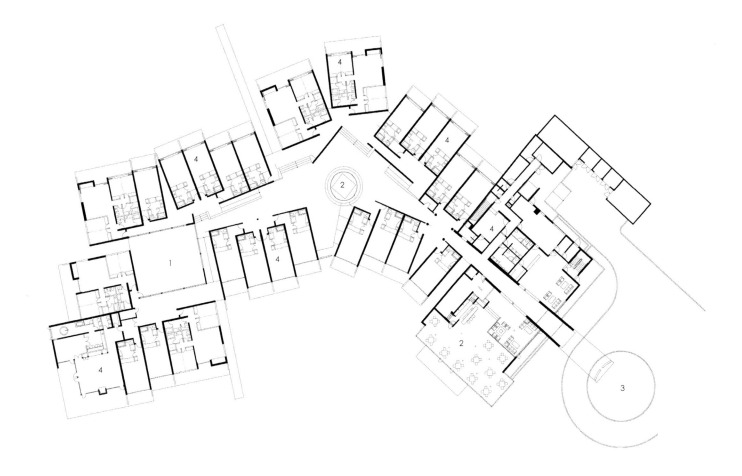

1. Bath pool
2. Lounge
3. Outdoor bath pool
4. Treatment room

Celebrity Solstice – AquaSpa

Location:
Miami, USA

Designer:
RTKL Associates Inc.

Photographer:
Patricia Parinejad

Completion date:
2008

More than five years ago, Celebrity Cruise Lines set out to develop a new class of vessel that would differentiate and position the company at the forefront of not only the cruise industry, but the hospitality world. Launched in 2008, Celebrity Solstice – designed to accommodate 2,850 passengers – creates an intimate and personalised hotel-like experience with the comforts and amenities of a land-based experience at sea.

Of the ship's diverse spaces, one of the most stunning is the two-level, 30,000-square-foot spa and solarium, a dynamic combination of form and function. Operating under a nationally recognised brand, the spa is one of the largest at sea, featuring 17 treatment rooms, a treatment suite, a thermal suite with two steam rooms, heated loungers with panoramic views, a full-service fitness centre, and relaxation lounge beds.

The design's colours and textures make reference to the Greek Isles. Deep blues and crisp whites – ocean-inspired colours – define the waiting areas and treatment rooms. Intricate mosaic tile patterns covering the walls and floors and a collection of heated lounge chairs feature varying combinations of the blue and white colour scheme and call to mind the serenity of a Mediterranean villa. For the more social hair and nail salon, RTKL selected a palette of bright fuchsias to accent the white

1.The treatment rooms are decorated with blue-flower patterns
2.The detail design of the massage beds and the wall
3.The interior colour is bright and warm
4.In the hair and nail salon, the palette of bright fuchsias accents the black and white interior space
5.The lounge
6.The elegant treatment room
7.The products area

walls and dark wood millwork. A monumental circular stair connects the spa's two levels, simplifying navigation and creating a sense of orientation for guests as they move between treatments.

RTKL worked closely with the ship's builders to create striking spaces that feature innovative use of materials and architectural forms. Every inch of the spa offers both artistic and functional expression, ensuring that each detail not only elevates the guest experience but sets a precedent for the cruise industry.

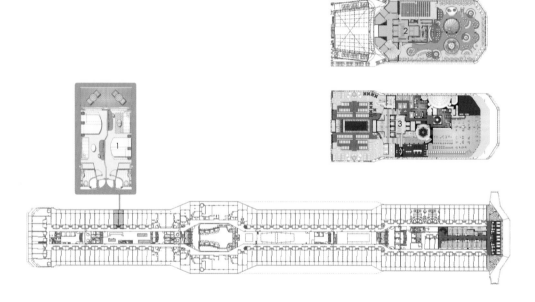

1. Typical treatment room
2. Lounge
3. Spa

4

5

Atomic Spa Suisse

Location:
Milan, Italy

Designer:
Simone Micheli

Photographer:
Jürgen Eheim

Completion date:
2009

This space possesses its personal identity independently of the hotel. The reception desk which is perfectly white and shiny gives us a warm welcome thanks to the multicolour backlighting and round shapes – it introduces us to the future world, the new enchanted world we are approaching by chasing a dreamlike and visionary Alice in Wonderland.

A round porthole which represents an eye on the future whispers us to get ready for a new experience, to raise our emotional antennas and prepare ourselves to perceive new and unpredictable sensations. From the full-length window which separates this area from the relaxation area we can glimpse through the screen printings a breathtaking display of lights and reflects, an outstanding array of plastic surfaces which strikes our senses and make them vibrating in awe. In the same way as an expert film director can convert experience into memory by increasing wait and desire following an ascending climax by means of a narrative rhythm pattern, Architect Simone Micheli diverts our attention from the sight of the incomplete central space in order to draw our attention along a long and narrow passage, a sort of emotional ascent towards the edge of sensory experience. This amazing trip is accompanied by luminous floating windows where products are exhibited on one side, while on the other side the acidated glass entrance doors of the treatment cabins are located.

1.The interior environment is fascinating
2.The eye-catching mirror bubbles
3.External view of the sauna
4.The mirror bubbles beside the bath pool
5.Guests can feel like in a magical world
6.The mirror bubbles lead guests into the spa
7.The figure decoration in bathroom is very unique

At the end of the passage just past the changing rooms soon after a few stairs featuring blue LEDs, we enter into the heart of the wellness centre. The mirror bubbles, the macroscopic plastic chromium plated "melted metal" drops hang from the ceiling and shine. As soon as these rarefied drops fulfill their task of accompanying the visitor in the same way as champagne bubbles go up the neck of the bottle, they thicken and they increase in number. As we approach the large swimming pool which metaphorically represents the origin of the lively explosion, they converge into a sudden burst of sparkling bubbles. The big sinuous trees having long swaying arms which seem to float in the air searching for a melting embrace form a Pantagruelian Ring a Ring o' Roses of phytomorphic souls by means of evocative reflects of the drops on the ceiling. All this creates a kaleidoscopic dreamlike scenery, enabling the visitor to enjoy a deep, unique sensory experience.

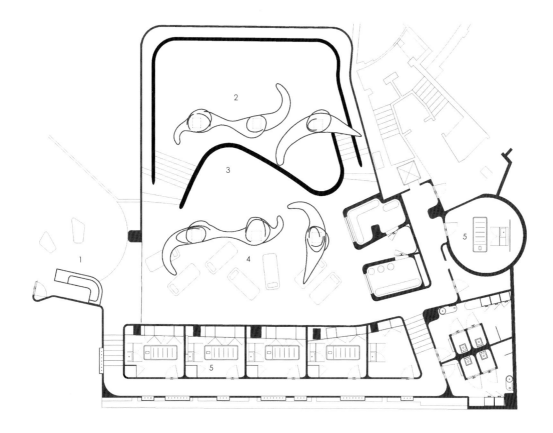

1. Reception
2. Bath pool
3. Shower
4. Relaxation area
5. Treatment room

4

5

Index